W9-AYO-699

Claire Chennault
Amelia Earhart
Charles Lindbergh
Eddie Rickenbacker
Manfred von Richthofen
Chuck Yeager

Chuck Yeager

Colleen Madonna Flood Williams

Philadelphia

Frontis: Chuck Yeager became the first pilot to break the sound barrier when he flew the X-1 over 700 miles per hour.

CHELSEA HOUSE PUBLISHERS

VP, NEW PRODUCT DEVELOPMENT Sally Cheney
DIRECTOR OF PRODUCTION Kim Shinners
CREATIVE MANAGER Takeshi Takahashi
MANUFACTURING MANAGER Diann Grasse

Staff for CHUCK YEAGER

EXECUTIVE EDITOR Lee Marcott
ASSOCIATE EDITOR Bill Conn
PRODUCTION EDITOR Jaimie Winkler
PHOTO EDITOR Sarah Bloom
COVER AND SERIES DESIGNER Keith Trego
LAYOUT 21st Century Publishing and Communications, Inc.

Printed and bound in the United States of America.

A Haights Cross Communications Company

http://www.chelseahouse.com

First Printing

1 3 5 7 9 8 6 4 2

Library of Congress Cataloging-in-Publication Data

Williams, Colleen Madonna Flood.
Chuck Yeager / Colleen Madonna Flood Williams.
p. cm. -- (Famous flyers)
Includes bibliographical references and index.
Contents: From shooting star to sinking star -- The early years -- World War II -- Breaking the sound barrier and beyond -- Pilots fly, astronauts ride -- The right stuff.
ISBN 0-7910-7216-9 (Hardcover) -- ISBN 0-7910-7500-1 (pbk.) 1. Yeager, Chuck, 1923---Juvenile literature. 2. Air pilots--United States--Biography--Juvenile literature. [1. Yeager, Chuck, 1923- 2. Air pilots.] I. Title. II. Series.
TL540.Y4W55 2003
623.74'6048'092--dc21

2003000827

CONTENTS

From Shooting Star to Sinking Star

In July of 1962, Chuck Yeager was selected to serve as commandant of the U.S. Air Force Aerospace Research Pilot School at Edwards Air Force Base in California. This assignment was a departure for Yeager, who was used to taking to the skies to push the boundaries of aviation himself. He was a veteran combat pilot from World War II, and the first pilot to break the sound barrier by flying at speeds of more than 700 miles per hour. While this position was not quite the hands-on type of assignment he was used to, it was certainly an exciting and important opportunity to be directly involved with the future of aerospace technology.

As commandant, Yeager was responsible for the training of U.S. military astronaut candidates. It was his job to keep an eye on the students as they went through the rigorous academic courses—like thermodynamics, bioastronautics, and Newtonian mechanics—as well as practical courses that taught the students the finer points of flying. The year-long program consisted of two phases: the first was the Experimental Test Pilot course, and the second was the Aerospace Research Pilot course. It was also Yeager's job to oversee the entire school staff.

By accepting the position as commandant of the U.S. Air Force Aerospace Research Pilot School at Edwards Air Force Base in California, Chuck Yeager placed himself at the cutting edge of aeronautical research. Experimental aircraft, like this Lunar Landing Research Vehicle, were not uncommon sights at the base.

At Edwards Air Force Base, Yeager worked closely with Paul F. Bikle, who was director of the National Aeronautics and Space Administration (NASA) Flight Research Center. As director of the NASA facility, Bikle was responsible for the flight operation of many major aeronautical research programs. Among these programs were the rocket-powered X-15 and the supersonic XB-70. Bikle was also involved with the research and development of the Lunar Landing Research Vehicle and wingless lifting bodies—predecessors of the space shuttle and reusable boosters.

Yeager and Bikle had worked together before. Bikle participated in early plans for the first powered flights made by the X-1—the plane Yeager would later fly when he broke the sound barrier, and the first plane in the line of aircraft that would eventually evolve into the space shuttle. Bikle had believed that the X-1 was destined for failure, but Yeager proved him wrong. So, Bikle and Yeager weren't strangers to one another—or to only being able to agree on disagreeing—when Bikle phoned Yeager to discuss the dry lakebed conditions of Smith's Ranch Lake one afternoon during 1965.

Dry lakebeds like Smith's Ranch Lake near Fallon, Nevada were important to NASA's research with high-speed planes like the X-15, which would reach speeds in excess of 4,500 miles per hour. These lakebeds provided the space supersonic jets needed to land, but they had to be bone dry or the plane would sink into the mud and possibly crash.

Bikle asked Yeager if he knew anything about the lakebed's condition, and Yeager told him that he had flown over it the day before in a B-57 and observed that the lakebed was wet. This, as both men understood, meant it was not a safe location for a landing. Yeager refused Bikle's request to attempt a landing, so Bikle asked him if he would at least fly over and survey the lake in one of NASA's airplanes with Neil Armstrong at the controls. Neil Armstrong was an

X-15 backup pilot at this time. Yeager agreed to take the flight as a passenger, as long as he was not held responsible for what occurred.

It was decided. Yeager would ride as a passenger with the then relatively unknown young astronaut trainee, Neil Armstrong, over to Smith's Ranch Lake to check the lakebed's conditions. Little did Yeager know that this decision would give birth to one of the most comical, and fortunately least damaging, incidents of his flying career.

The X-15

The X-15 was the result of a joint research program subsidized by the National Advisory Committee for Aeronautics, the U.S. Air Force, the U.S. Navy, and private industry. North American was selected as the prime contractor on the project. Hence, the X-15 is also very commonly known as the North American X-15.

The X-15 was a high-speed research aircraft first flown on June 8, 1959. It was used to research the effects of thermal heating and atmospheric reentry on winged aircraft. The United States used the X-15 to test life support systems for spacecraft. It was also used to study aircraft control and stability at high speeds.

The X-15 holds both the speed record of Mach 6.72, or 4,534 mph, and the altitude record of 67.08 miles, or 354,200 feet, for a winged aircraft. The aircraft is 50 feet, 7 inches long, 13 feet tall, and weighs 12,500 pounds when it is empty of all fuel, according to the Smithsonian National Air and Space Museum.

The X-15 was manufactured using an exceptionally strong nickel alloy, called Inconel X. This nickel alloy was used to ensure that the aircraft could survive the temperatures of up to 1,200°F that it might encounter at exceptionally high speeds.

The X-15 was air-launched from a Boeing B-52 Stratofortress aircraft, its so-called "mother plane." The launch occurred at an elevation of 45,000 feet and a speed of 500 mph. The pilot would then fly the plane along a prearranged path, until arriving at and landing on the clay soil of Roger's Dry Lake.

Only three X-15 aircraft were built. They were named, simply, the X-15-1, the X-15-2, and the X-15-3. The aircraft were used in a total of 199 research flights.

Yeager arrived at NASA with his chute and helmet in hand, where he met with Neil Armstrong. For their flight, Armstrong had prepped a T-33. T-33s were used for training pilots who had already proven themselves capable of flying propeller-driven aircraft. A T-33 was basically a teacher's version of a single-seat F-80 fighter plane with an extra long fuselage. The extended fuselage of the T-33 accommodated a second cockpit, which could be used by a teacher to observe a student in action. With a maximum speed of 525 mph and a cruising speed of 455 mph, these planes—particularly their single-seat F-80 alter egos—were often referred to as "Shooting Stars."

Yeager attempted to talk Armstrong out of flying over to the lakebed, but Armstrong was determined to fly over it and give it a quick look. Armstrong told Yeager that he'd just test the surface of the lakebed by performing a light "touch-and-go." This meant he'd put the wheels of the T-33 down, and then quickly hit the throttle and soar back up into the sky. Or so Armstrong had planned, anyway.

Yeager advised Armstrong that the T-33 was far too heavy for such a maneuver. The plane, after all, was carrying the combined weight of a passenger and a great deal of fuel. He did not think the T-33 had enough power to handle such a situation given the potentially muddy conditions of the lakebed, and he told Armstrong this in no uncertain terms. Yeager knew that if they attempted to perform a touch-and-go type of landing, the wet lakebed would most certainly just suck them in, making it impossible to take back off once they had touched down. Still, the headstrong Armstrong was convinced he could perform the maneuver with no difficulties.

Dressed in light flying suits and gloves, Armstrong and Yeager took off towards the lakebed. It was approximately 250 miles from the base to the lake, but the T-33 made the trip in approximately 30 minutes. When they were close enough to observe the lakebed conditions, the men could not have disagreed more on what they both saw. Yeager remarked immediately that the lakebed was too wet and muddy to do anything more than fly over it and return back to base, but Armstrong believed that it was dry enough for a touch-and-go. He was determined to take the risk despite the voice of experience coming from the second cockpit of the T-33.

Armstrong flew in toward the lakebed. He touched down with the T-33 and the aircraft began to decelerate. Hitting the throttle, Armstrong applied full power, but the T-33 was sinking into the mud of the very wet "dry" lakebed. They were stuck. The "Shooting Star" was now a "Sinking Star." Yeager had been right, but as the plane sunk and threatened to flip, being right was very little consolation to him.

The plane came to a stop without further incident, leaving the two men stuck in the mud in middle of nowhere. They were nearly 30 miles from the closest road and it was late in the afternoon. The sun would be setting in just a few hours. Neither man was dressed warmly. Their lightweight, thin flying suits provided little protection from the cold weather, and it was bound to get pretty cold and uncomfortable if they had to spend much time stuck where they were. There were definitely better places to be.

There they sat, on the wing of the sinking T-33.

Looking down, neither man could help but notice the now very apparent wet conditions of the dry lakebed. The mud was thick and gooey. The T-33 was good and stuck. Yeager could not have been more right, or Armstrong more wrong.

Paul Bikle had sensed there might be a problem. Despite their tendency to disagree, he knew that Yeager had spent a lot of time flying over and landing on the dry lakebeds around the Edwards Air Force Base area. After all, Yeager had been flying in this area since 1945. He also knew that if Yeager had said the lakebed was wet, and Yeager had flown over it just a day before they had spoken, then he was probably

A young backup X-15 pilot named Neil Armstrong was at Edwards Air Force Base at the same time as Chuck Yeager. The two men teamed up for an observation flight over Smith's Ranch Lake to check the conditions of the lakebed.

right. Bikle knew, too, that Armstrong wanted to try a touch-and-go on what he believed were safe lakebed conditions. It was a well-known fact that the astronauts didn't think much of military pilots and military pilots returned the favor; as an astronaut trainee, Armstrong was bound to disagree with an old military pilot like Yeager. In order to be sure the two men were all right, Bikle had ordered a Gooney Bird to follow them.

A Gooney Bird is a C-47, which was adapted for use by the military from the 1937 DC-3 commercial airliners. The military began ordering C-47s in 1940 and had over 9,000 of the airplanes by the end of World War II. American soldiers nicknamed it the "gooney bird." The C-47 had a long and illustrious career as a military aircraft. During World War II, Gooney Birds carried personnel and cargo, towed troop-carrying gliders, and dropped paratroops behind enemy lines. In Korea and Vietnam, the slow moving planes were used to haul wounded troops to safety, to drop flares to light the way for troops during night attacks, to conduct reconnaissance missions, and to perform flying ground attack missions. Now, the Gooney Bird was Chuck Yeager's and Neil Armstrong's only hope for being pulled out of the mud of Smith's Ranch Lake.

Yeager and Armstrong saw the Gooney Bird approaching and sprung into action, climbing back into the downed plane. Yeager flicked the battery switch to turn on the radio and call to the Gooney Bird's pilot. Yeager and the pilot decided upon a course of action as quickly as they could.

Armstrong and Yeager hurriedly made their way to the edge of the lakebed. Their feet sunk deep into the mud with each and every step they took. Behind them, they left a trail of wet mushy footprints. The pilot landed along the edge of the lakebed and kept the C-47 rolling along with its door open. Yeager and Armstrong ran up to the moving plane and jumped into the back end of the C-47. In order to keep from

Fortunately, both Chuck Yeager (seen here) and Neil Armstrong walked away from the T-33 crash in the lakebed with nothing more than a funny story to tell their fellow pilots. It wasn't Chuck's first brush with death in an airplane, and it wouldn't be his last.

sinking, the pilot of the Gooney Bird had to keep that plane in motion. Fortunately for all parties concerned, although the Gooney Bird left a great furrow in the lakebed, it did not sink. The pilot was able to keep his power and get back up off the ground.

It was night time when the men arrived back at Edwards Air Force Base. The T-33 was still stuck in the mud back at Smith's Ranch Lake. That T-33 would sit there, stuck in the mud for a week, until the Navy sent a recovery team out to rescue it.

Neither man was any worse for the wear, but Armstrong's pride surely must have been hurt. To this day, Yeager jests about the incident. In one interview, he remarked wryly, "Neil was a pretty good engineer. He wasn't too good an airplane driver."

The Early Years

Chuck Yeager was born on February 13, 1923. His mother, Susie Mae Yeager, was a hearty, religious woman of French and Dutch descent. His father, Albert Hal Yeager, was German and Dutch. Al was a hard working man with massive arms. But bigger than his muscular arms were his opinions and convictions.

Chuck was the second of the Yeager children, born about fifteen months after his big brother, Roy. The Yeagers were living in Myra, West Virginia at the time of Chuck's birth, but soon moved to Hubble, West Virginia, where Al Yeager worked for the railroad. The family moved again shortly thereafter and settled in Hamlin, West Virginia, where Al went to work drilling for natural gas.

Although Hamlin, West Virginia was a small town, it was big compared to Myra. Hamlin had a population of approximately 600 during the late 1920s and early 1930s. The residents of the rural town depended upon farming, logging, natural gas drilling, and coal mining industries to make their livings.

The Yeagers settled into life in Hamlin, not knowing that

Towns like Hamlin, West Virginia—where Chuck spent his childhood—were poor in good times, and even poorer when the Great Depression hit. But the Yeagers were resourceful and made do with the little that they had.

tragedy loomed ahead. The young family happily nestled into a small clapboard house that was located across from the local elementary school. Roy, Chuck, and their two-year-old baby sister, Doris Ann, kept Susie Mae busy while Al traveled from jobsite to jobsite drilling for natural gas in West Virginia and Kentucky.

Unfortunately for the Yeager family, an unspeakable tragedy struck the young family during one holiday season. Roy and Chuck were playing with their father's shotgun, when Roy loaded the 12 gauge and inadvertently fired it. The bullet struck Doris Ann, killing her.

In his autobiography, *Yeager*, Chuck explains how his father reacted to the incident by teaching his two young sons about gun safety. From then on, the family never discussed the incident. In his book, Yeager explains, "That's the Yeager way; we keep our hurts to ourselves."

Times were not easy for the Yeager family. When money was scarce, Susie Mae cooked very plain meals of white corn-meal and served it with milk and sugar quite frequently. When times were even tougher, the family lived on corn bread and buttermilk. The Yeager boys did not have much in the way of material things, but they had their parents and they had each other.

When the Great Depression hit the nation, Al Yeager managed to keep working in the gas fields. Hard times were not new to the Yeagers. The young West Virginian family already knew what it was like to be poor. In typical Yeager family style, not only did the Yeagers survive the depression, the growing family somehow even managed to buy a house during those hard years. Signing a mortgage for $1,800, Al Yeager moved his family into a two-story house. The mortgage included the house's accompanying two little city blocks. With its four bedrooms and two small city blocks, the house and yard were more than big enough for the Yeagers.

The family planted a garden, raised chickens, hogs, and even kept a cow. Susie Mae pickled corn and beans and made sauerkraut for her family. For sweeter treats, Susie Mae made apple butter with peppermint flavoring and boiled sorghum molasses for syrup.

Roy and Chuck helped slaughter hogs so that Susie Mae could make ham and cure bacon. The boys harvested nuts and berries from the local forests. They cheerfully hunted for edible plants like paw paws and wild persimmons.

Roy and Chuck learned to entertain themselves in the great West Virginian outdoors. Together the two boys built forts, climbed trees, flew kites, and explored the surrounding

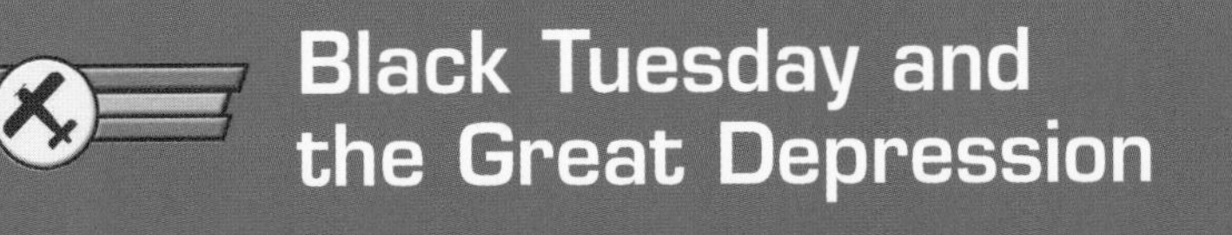

Black Tuesday and the Great Depression

October 29, 1929, is generally referred to as "Black Tuesday"—the day the stock market crashed and the Great Depression began. Just a few days earlier, on October 24, 1929, the stock market began to fluctuate greatly. People started dumping their stocks into the market and selling them as quickly as possible.

To stabilize the stock market and the American economy, J.P. Morgan and several other wealthy financiers attempted to buy up a great deal of the stock that was being sold. At first, it seemed that they had achieved their goal—on Friday, October 25, 1929, the stock market seemed to have stabilized. Unfortunately, when the stock market reopened for business on Monday, October 28, 1929, people once again began selling their stocks. The public was openly panicking. Almost everyone wanted to get rid of whatever stocks they had.

On Black Tuesday, prices on the stock market dropped so low that, within the first few hours of the day, stockbrokers had witnessed the cancellation of all the gains that had been made in the previous year. Between October 29, 1929, and November 13, 1929, stock prices continued to drop. From October 29, 1929 until the United States entered World War II in 1941, thousands of banks went out of business and millions of savings accounts were lost. Unemployment led to widespread poverty and hunger throughout the United States. This period is referred to as "The Great Depression."

countryside. Their outdoor adventures helped to put food on the table as well as to keep the two growing boys busy. They hunted rabbits and squirrels in the hills and fished for suckers and bass in the Mud River.

To this day, Chuck Yeager is fond of relating how he was often fifteen or so minutes late for school. As a young man, he often rose early to do a bit of squirrel hunting before the school bell rang. According to Yeager's nostalgic accounts of childhood days gone by, squirrel skinning was not an excuse the principal considered valid for tardiness.

The two older Yeager boys were expected to do many household chores, since Al Yeager was away in the gas fields most of the time and Susie Mae's hands were full. The hard-working mother always seemed to be cooking and cleaning in addition to caring for the family, particularly after the births of Pansy Lee and Hal, Jr.

Every Saturday night, Susie Mae supervised the Yeager children as they washed up before Sunday-school classes. The boys ran barefoot most of the time, so their feet were generally extremely dirty by the end of the week. On Sundays, however, the Yeagers wore shoes to Sunday school and to church. Sunday nights, their feet would be clean, but tired and sore from wearing their Sunday-school shoes.

The family attended Hamlin's Northern Methodist Church. This was the church for the Republican Methodist minority of Hamlin, West Virginia. The Democrats, who were the majority, attended Hamlin's Southern Methodist Church. The Methodists of Hamlin did not separate church and state affairs.

Chuck's elementary school years started off with a bang but went out with more of a whimper. He was advanced from the first to third grade, skipping the second grade entirely. Unfortunately, this advancement was canceled out by the reputation he built as a fifth grader. He repeated the grade, and graduated with his original class.

Among his memories of his early school days, Yeager has revealed that he particularly remembers having to read a book entitled, *Crooked Bill.* At the time, he was in the fourth or fifth grade and had to give a book report on the story. Yeager recalls this book report as being one of the toughest things he had ever had to do up to that point in his life. True to his mountain and backwoods nature, he also remembers enjoying books that dealt with wildlife, like those written by Jack London.

During his high school years, Chuck excelled at typing and math. He typed 60 words per minute, a foreshadowing of the excellent hand-eye coordination and manual dexterity that would make him such a great pilot. English and History were not his better subjects. He took up the trombone and joined the county's school band. He played football and basketball, but his real loves were pool and ping-pong.

Like most other teenaged boys, Chuck spent his fair share of time chasing girls. By his own accounts, during his senior year, he caught one or two of them, too! Chuck took to staying out late on dates with some of the girls in his class. When his mom protested his late hours by locking him out of the house, Chuck relied on the skills he had learned during his early childhood tree-climbing days. He simply scrambled up a tree and entered his bedroom through a second story window.

From his earliest childhood years, Chuck excelled in the world of mechanics. His childhood afforded him many chances to develop his mechanical skills, and he spent a great deal of time with his father learning about the tools of the gas-drilling trade.

Together, Chuck, his father, and brother Roy overhauled engines. The two eldest Yeager brothers learned how to run

Chuck excelled at a few subjects in school, like Mathematics, but always had difficulty with English and History. He did, however, enjoy writers like Jack London (pictured here) who told stories about outdoor adventurers.

water and gasoline pumps. They watched as their dad taught them the art of "dressing" drilling bits.

Between his dad and the Ford and Hager automobile

garages in town, Yeager learned enough to know that "a machine will bite a person who does not understand it." The Ford and Hager garages of Hamlin were each a sort of homespun vocational training ground for Hamlin high school boys with an interest in mechanics. Yeager's days spent working with machines under the watchful eyes of Shorty Hager and Carl Clay of the Ford garage taught him how to " . . . push a machine without it biting me."

By the time Chuck graduated from high school, he could take an engine apart and put it back together again. This skill, coupled with his natural expert marksmanship with a gun, would contribute greatly to his success in the military. And his personality was ideally suited to life as a soldier as well.

Good old fashioned values and morals obtained from his parents helped to shape and prepare that personality. Both of his parents were shining examples of the persistent pioneer spirit. Susie Mae and Al Yeager were hard working, honest, and honorable. When the Yeagers gave their word, they always stood by it.

Al, in particular, was known for his stubbornness. Chuck inherited this stubborn streak from his father and it would be just this type of stubborn stick-to-itiveness that would save his life during World War II. Another gift Chuck Yeager received from his humble but hearty upbringing was the belief that any job worth doing was worth doing well.

In 1941, Chuck grabbed his high school diploma and his birth certificate and used them to gain entrance to the United States Army Air Corps. He enlisted for two years. He left home with these simple words of fatherly advice ringing in his ears: "Son, don't gamble."

The young Chuck had enlisted to become an army mechanic, a goal he quickly accomplished. Yeager was not, at the time that he had joined the service, infatuated with airplanes. He was much more focused on simply being

This recruiting poster for the U.S. Army Air Forces enticed many young men like Chuck to enlist. Chuck joined the Army Air Corps to become an airplane mechanic, with no real intention of ever leaving the ground.

the best mechanic that he could possibly be. Soon, he was not only a mechanic, but a crew chief.

He hadn't joined the service to fly airplanes. In fact, up until he joined the service and became trained as an airplane mechanic, he had only been really close to one airplane in his life. The first airplane Chuck Yeager ever saw close up was one that had made an emergency landing about a mile from the Yeagers' home. A typical teenager, when Chuck heard about the plane that had landed in the neighboring cornfield, the then fifteen- or sixteen-year-old boy rode his bike on over to take a look. Yeager has remarked that he simply took a look at it and then left. What else was there for a country boy from a town like Hamlin to do in such a situation?

Evidently the incident did not make a huge impression on him at the time because when he talks about it now he refers to the plane as "a cub or something." He admits, too, quite openly that he wasn't very impressed by it. After all, he was only fifteen or sixteen at the time, and didn't really know much about what he was looking at in that cornfield.

Still, in late November of 1941, an announcement on an army bulletin board caught the young West Virginian's eye. The memo explained that a program referred to as the "Flying Sergeant's Program" was opening. Under this program, if you were 18, had a high school diploma, and could pass a physical, then you could apply to enter flight school to be trained to become a flying sergeant.

Here was a program that not only allowed you to learn to fly, but also got you out of KP (kitchen patrol) duty! The young crew chief put in his application. He took a physical early in December of 1941. Now, all there was left to do was wait for his results.

Just a few days later, the Japanese bombed Pearl Harbor. A saddened but determined United States pulled together to

The Attack on Pearl Harbor

Japan's infamous attack on Pearl Harbor began sometime around 8 A.M. on December 7, 1941. The attack caught the United States by complete surprise. Admiral Yamamoto, a Japanese superior officer, masterminded the devastatingly effective Japanese Imperial Navy attack. Following Yamamoto's plan, over 350 Japanese naval aircraft, led by Commander Mitsuo Fuchido, bombed select targets in Oahu, Hawaii.

The first attack targeted the Army Air Forces' Wheeler and Hickam Fields. The goal of this strike was to gain air control by destroying as many grounded U.S. fighter planes as possible. Unfortunately, the U.S. aircraft were sitting ducks. Parked in neat rows, wingtip to wingtip, the planes could not have been easier targets. The Japanese attack destroyed almost all of the war planes it targeted.

The attack was also designed to damage and destroy as many U.S. aircraft carriers and battleships as possible. Fortunately for the United States, many of the nation's ships were out to sea. The Japanese strike took its toll, but it was nowhere near as devastating as Admiral Yamamoto had hoped. Many of the ships would be repaired and live to fight another day. Unfortunately, the USS *Arizona*, the USS *Utah*, and the USS *Oklahoma* would never sail again.

The *Oklahoma*, a battleship, was struck by an estimated five or more torpedoes. It rolled over, trapping sailors deep within its hull. An eerie metallic tapping sound could be heard issuing an SOS from deep within the ship. The following day, 32 men were rescued from the belly of the great battleship. They had taken turns banging on the ship's hull with a wrench to attract the attention of rescuers.

The *Utah* was an old battleship that was at that time being employed as a target ship. It was struck by Japanese bombers who thought it was an aircraft carrier. The *Utah* was walloped by two torpedoes, and capsized almost immediately in response to the blows. Over 50 men perished along with the *Utah*. Some were struck down by Japanese bullets, others drowned as the ship capsized.

The *Arizona* exploded as an armor-piercing bomb dropped from the sky above, igniting over a million pounds of gunpowder aboard the vessel. Broken in two, the ship sunk to the bottom of the harbor in less than ten minutes.

Within two hours, 21 United States ships were sunk or damaged. Three-fourths of the military planes in Hawaii were hit. Most heartrending of all, over 2,400 civilians and military personnel were killed in the attack. Still, the Japanese had not achieved their greatest goal. The people of the United States are far from demoralized. They are outraged. The nation pulled together swiftly with only one thing on its mind: victory against the Japanese and all who stand with them.

enter World War II. The year ended with no word of Chuck's application's status. Airplane mechanic and crew chief Chuck Yeager would have to wait to see if he was going to receive a pay raise, a promotion, and a shot at pilot school. Little did he know, at the time, that he had all of that and much more in store for him.

World War II

Over six months later, the young mechanic from the mountains of West Virginia received new orders. It was official. Chuck Yeager had been accepted into the Flying Sergeant's Program. In September of 1942, Chuck entered pilot training school.

Chuck had flown in airplane only once with a flight maintenance officer. He had serviced the plane, and the kind officer had offered to take him up for a ride. The officer had to check the plane out anyway, so taking young Chuck along with him wouldn't really be a problem or inconvenience to anyone. Or so the officer must have thought.

Chuck went along for the ride, all right. Unfortunately, it didn't agree with him one bit. He vomited all over the passenger seat!

Now, here he was, a young enlisted mechanic, who'd thrown up during his first ride in an airplane, and he was entering pilot school. But, amazingly, within just a few months of entering the

Flying Sergeant's Program, it was obvious to all who watched him that Chuck Yeager was a natural pilot.

In March of 1943, he graduated as an enlisted flight officer at Luke Field, Arizona. His brother Hal and father proudly attended the ceremony and watched as he was given his wings. He not only completed the program, but also was recommended to go on and become a fighter pilot.

Chuck was then assigned to the 363rd Fighter Squadron (357th Fighter Group) and stationed at Tonopah, Nevada. In Nevada, he started fighter training in a Bell P-39 Airacobra. The Airacobra was commonly known among the troops as just simply the P-39.

While Chuck liked flying the Bell P-39 Airacobra, most pilots dreaded flying it so much that they created a disparaging song about it. The Airacobra had a rear-mounted engine that made it unwieldy and dangerous.

Although Yeager himself enjoyed it, the Airacobra was not a well-liked aircraft. Most flyers dreaded having to fly the P-39. It was disliked by so many pilots that it inspired some to sing about it:

> Don't give me a P-39,
> With an engine that's mounted behind.
> It will tumble and roll
> and dig a big hole,
> Don't give me a P-39.

In June of 1943, Chuck was sent to Santa Rosa to begin bomber escort and coastal patrol operations training. Shortly after that, he received orders to report to Wright Field in Ohio. He was needed to serve as a test pilot.

His duties at Wright Field primarily revolved around the testing of a new propeller for the P-39. Still, he managed to find some free time. He used this time to test out another, bigger plane—the P-47 fighter.

Chuck took that P-47 and flew to Hamlin. He buzzed the entire town, knowing that they'd figure out it was him. After all, he was the only fighter pilot from Hamlin. Folks knew it was him, all right. At first, however, they were none too pleased with Chuck's antics and the disturbance he brought to their normally peaceful town. Some were downright angry about the whole affair. Still, Chuck was persistent, and eventually they got used to him buzzing the small West Virginia town.

Eventually, Chuck was ordered to return to his unit. He met up with them just in time to be transferred to Oroville, California. It was in Oroville that Chuck met Glennis Dickhouse, the love of his life. For two months, Chuck and Glennis dated and grew close to one another.

Next came the last phase of their fighter pilot training in Casper, Wyoming. Their free time in Casper proved to be a lot of fun. There were deer and antelope galore. The young pilots hunted them from the skies, herding them with their aircraft and then shooting them from the sky. Many a night, the men of the 363rd Fighter Squadron enjoyed fresh roasts and steaks of antelope or deer meat.

On October 23, 1943, Chuck suffered his first true brush with death in an aircraft. His engine blew up during a high-speed flight exercise. As his plane burst into flames, Chuck was forced to bail out of it. To add insult to injury, he was knocked unconscious when his parachute opened.

Luckily, a sheepherder found the injured pilot. With the help of a burro, the sheepherder was able to get the injured Yeager to safety. The sheepherder simply threw Chuck's body across the burro's back and headed for help. Chuck suffered a fractured spine and was hospitalized so he could recover from his injuries. When reminiscing about the event, Chuck mentions that not only did he end up in a lot of pain with a fractured back, but he missed a scheduled rendezvous with Glennis in Reno, too.

In November of 1943, just before Chuck's unit was sent to England, he and Glennis promised to write one another. Chuck was sent overseas and he began flying combat missions in a P-51 Mustang. Chuck named each and every plane he flew during World War II *Glamorous Glen*, after his sweetheart back in Oroville.

When he first arrived overseas, Chuck flew seven successful combat missions. On his seventh mission, he shot down a Messerschmitt. His eighth combat mission was not as successful, unfortunately. On that fateful eighth combat flight, the flyboy from Hamlin was shot down. His plane was attacked by three German FW-190s, and he had no choice but to bail out of his destroyed aircraft. Chuck landed in occupied France about fifty miles from Bordeaux.

It was Sunday, March 5, 1944. The twenty-one-year-old's hands and feet were perforated with shards of shrapnel. His right calf had a hole in it, and his forehead was cut. Sewn into his flight suit was a silk map of Europe. He studied it and discovered that he was very close to a French town named Angouleme. But he would have to cross the Pyrenees and get into Spain to escape the Germans first.

He could hear the buzz of low-flying German aircraft

The Mustang

Approximately 3,888 P-51 B/C Mustangs were produced. They were armed with four .50-caliber machine guns and two 1,000-pound bombs. Sporting Packard V-1650-3.7 Merlin engines, these planes could fly as fast as 440 mph at 30,000 feet.

The Mustang was 32 feet, 3 inches long, and a little over 13 feet tall. The fighter plane had a wingspan of 37 feet and a wing area of approximately 237 square feet.

Empty, the aircraft weighed a little less than 7,000 pounds. Its normal takeoff weight, however, was over 9,000 pounds. The Merlin-powered B and C P-51 Mustangs were outstanding high-altitude performance aircraft.

Their great range capabilities also stood out as exceptional among other fighter planes of the era. The combination of superior performance and range capability soon distinguished the Mustangs as a fighter pilot's first choice among available planes.

The Mustang did have a few drawbacks, however. Its original canopy had very restricted visibility. This was very dangerous, since a fighter pilot needed to be able to see the enemy before the enemy saw him. Secondly, the plane's four machine guns often jammed. Pilots complained, too, that the four .50-caliber machine guns just did not provide enough firepower. So, the P-51 D was developed in response to these complaints.

The P-51 D had better visibility. This was achieved by using a cut-down aft fuselage section and a full bubble canopy. It also had six machine guns instead of four. To improve their performance, the machine guns on a P-51 D were mounted upright. Previously, machine guns in the Mustang had been mounted at a slant, which added to the likelihood of ammunition jams.

The P-51 D Mustang, and the very similar P-51 K Mustang, served in combat in World War II for almost a year. The planes' sleek design, improved firepower and visibility, as well as their high-speed and long-range capacities served the United States and her allies quite well. Perhaps that is why, even today, the Mustang remains an aircraft that is near and dear to most fighter pilots' hearts.

A group of German FW-190 fighter-bombers broke Chuck's lucky streak when they shot him down during his eighth mission. Chuck crash landed, broken and bruised, in German-occupied France with a new mission—to get safely over the Pyrenees into Spain.

searching for him. He hunkered down in the thick brush, out of sight of the enemy, waiting for night to fall. Under the cover of darkness he raided a nearby farm field and gathered some potatoes and turnips for nourishment. He realized, however, that it was best to stay put.

Shortly before nightfall, it started to rain. Cold and wet, Chuck searched for the chocolate bar from his survival kit. After devouring it with the potatoes and turnips, he curled up under his parachute and tried to get some sleep.

The first light of morning found Chuck tired but alert, and holding his pistol as he watched a local woodcutter making his way through the woods. The man was carrying a heavy axe, the tool of his trade. The young pilot decided to make a move. Attacking from behind, Yeager forced the woodcutter to drop the axe. The frightened Frenchman stared in disbelief as the wild American flyboy waved a pistol in his face. The woodcutter spoke no English, and Chuck spoke no French.

Fortunately, the two men were able to communicate enough to realize that they were allies and not enemies, and they formed a plan. The Frenchman would get help and return with someone who spoke English. The young pilot would stay behind, remain in hiding, and stay quiet.

The woodcutter disappeared, leaving his axe behind for Chuck, who found a new hiding place in a group of lofty trees. He hoped the woodcutter would not return with a squad of German soldiers.

Luck was on Chuck's side. The woodcutter returned with an old man who spoke excellent English. They were going to help Chuck, but first, they had to get him safely out of the forest. There were German soldiers everywhere, beating the brush in search of the downed American pilot. They searched the treetops for his parachute, and neighboring farmhouses and fields where he may have been hiding.

The woodcutter and the old man led Chuck to a small farmhouse, and took him into a barn and then up into its hayloft. In the hayloft, there was a small tool closet. They quickly put the young pilot into the closet, locked it, and then covered it with hay.

Shortly afterwards, the farm was swarming with German soldiers. From his hiding spot in the tool closet, Chuck could hear their voices. They were in the hayloft, searching for him in the hay. Chuck held his breath and tightened his grip on his gun. They could discover him at any given moment.

A few hours later, the old man returned, ensuring Chuck that the Germans were gone and he was safe. The old man brought a doctor with him to examine Chuck's wounds, and the French family who owned the farmhouse fed and sheltered him for approximately a week before it was safe enough to move.

Dressed like a woodcutter with an axe strapped on his back,

Chuck lived and worked with a group of French *Maquis* guerrillas while waiting for the snow and ice in the Pyrenees to melt. The *Maquis'* fighting tactics involved nighttime raids against the Nazis during their occupation of France.

Chuck bicycled with the doctor to another farmhouse in the town of Nerac, just outside of Roquefort. In Nerac, he stayed in a shed on the property of a farm owned by a farmer named Gabriel, with Gabriel's wife and son. After some time passed, it was once again time to move. Gabriel took Chuck deep into the pine forest, and told him to wait. Many hours later, Gabriel returned, but he was not alone.

The farmer was accompanied by a group of men wearing black berets on their heads and sashes like bandoliers of rifle cartridges across their chests. The men were part of the *Maquis*—a group French resistance fighters.

It was explained to the young pilot that it was too snowy to cross the Pyrenees at that time, and he would have to wait until the snow thawed. When there was less snow in the mountain passes, he would be able to try to escape into Spain. In the meantime, however, he would have to live and work with the

Maquis. From that point on, he would have to follow in the footsteps of the Maquis.

The French freedom fighters would hide by day and attack at night—the Maquis were famous for sabotaging German supply routes. They ambushed small motorized convoys, destroyed whole sections of railroad track, and blew up trains that were carrying German military equipment and munitions.

At first, the tight-knit group was wary of the young American. Chuck was relegated to simple chores like tending to the group's cow or helping to butcher meat. But after a while, the group warmed up to the young fighter pilot, and he was invited to accompany them on a supply mission.

Included in the supplies that they received were fuses, explosives, and timing devices. Since Chuck had grown up helping his dad set off plastic explosives as part of his job as a gas driller, he explained to the leader of the Maquis that he could help them use the explosives effectively. He became the Maquis' demolitions expert.

In March, Chuck was taken on a mission into town, a mission that he knew could turn out to be quite dangerous. The French towns were overrun with Vichy conspirators and German soldiers. Neither a French Resistance member nor a downed American pilot would ever want to run into members of either the German military or the Vichy government—torture and death were very real possible outcomes of such an encounter.

But before reaching town, Chuck was met by a van and he was ordered to get inside. It was the perfect time to attempt to travel across the Pyrenees and escape into Spain, but he had to leave immediately.

It was March 23 when the van dropped Chuck and three others off at the starting point of their journey into Spain. The men were all given knapsacks filled with supplies and maps. It was dark. They were told to walk about one hundred yards until they came upon a woodsman's shed, where they should spend the night before beginning their journey at dawn.

It would be a dangerous journey across treacherous mountain passes patrolled by German soldiers. The weather would be cold and the wind would add to the freezing temperatures. One of the men accompanying Chuck was a lieutenant who served as a navigator on a downed B-24 bomber. Chuck and the lieutenant walked together as they approached the timberline of the mountains. Unfortunately, Chuck and the lieutenant were eventually forced to leave the other two escapees because they could not keep up over the difficult mountain passes.

The two men trudged through snow that sometimes reached as high as their knees. Their feet and legs were wet and cold. Icy ridges forced them to sit and slide down passes from time to time, and the thin mountain air forced them to stop and rest every fifteen minutes to catch their breath. The journey was anything but easy.

Tired, wet, and cold, the two soldiers stumbled onto a cabin. Cautiously, with guns readied, they opened the cabin door. It was empty, and offered them the perfect place to rest and sleep, sleep that would quickly be interrupted by the sound of gun fire. They had been discovered, tracked by the Germans who were now firing round after round through the front door of the cabin.

The two men scrambled to the back of the cabin and out a window; the lieutenant was hit, but there was no time to assess the severity of his wound. The two men slid down the treacherous mountainside, covering miles in what seemed like minutes—pushed forward by ice, snow, and gravity. They finally landed with a splash in a deep mountain stream.

The lieutenant was bleeding badly, shot in the leg. His lower leg was hanging onto his knee by just a tendon. A dumdum bullet—which expands when it strikes its target—had found its mark and had torn the lieutenant's lower leg to shreds.

Chuck wrapped the stump of the lieutenant's knee with a silk remnant from his parachute. One of the Frenchmen's wives who had helped him had sewn his parachute into a shirt for him. It was now a bandage for a wounded fellow American.

The two men were well hidden from the Germans, but they were now even colder and wetter than before they entered the cabin to sleep—and at the mercy of the elements. The lieutenant with Chuck was in real danger of dying from his wound. Still, there was nothing for them to do but bide their time. It was daylight and they did not dare risk moving back up the mountainside yet.

Night fell and Chuck began dragging the lieutenant back up the mountain. The deadweight of 170 pounds made the climb excruciatingly difficult. Finally, they reached the top. In the distance, they could see a road that was within the borders of Spain. They made it.

Exhausted by the time he reached the road, Chuck propped the lieutenant's now gray body at the side of the road. He hoped someone would find him and help him in time, if it was not already too late. With that, Yeager headed off to the south in search of a town.

The lieutenant did, indeed, survive. He was picked up by the Guardia Civil—Spain's national public security force—and transported to a nearby hospital. After a bit of time in the hospital, he was sent home to the United States.

Chuck, on the other hand, hiked another twenty miles. He reached a small town and contacted the local authorities. But instead of helping him, the Spanish police threw him in jail!

The American flyboy took exception to this treatment, as he had been through far too much to end up in jail. Using his survival kit's saw, he cut through the brass bars of his cell window. Too tired to run far, he made his way to a nearby hotel.

The police didn't bother him for some reason, although it was a small town and they knew exactly where he had gone. At the hotel, Yeager dined on chicken and beans. He took a warm bath and climbed into bed. It was March 28, 1944—over twenty days since he was shot down.

On March 30, 1944, the American consul arrived at Chuck's hotel. It took approximately a month, but the consul was able to negotiate the release of Chuck and several other evaders from Spain. The war had created a gasoline shortage, so the United States traded gallons of Texaco's finest to the gasoline-hungry Spanish government in exchange for the release of their flyboys.

By May, Chuck was back in England. The men of his squadron welcomed him back, slightly in awe—he was the first downed pilot that they had ever seen make it back from behind enemy lines.

Tanned from the Spanish sun and slightly heavier than when he had been shot down, the young pilot was an anomaly. Instead of looking like a thin, sickly prisoner of war, Chuck returned to his squadron looking as if he had just returned from a vacation. In a manner of speaking, he had just returned from a brief vacation in Spain. Uncle Sam had been picking up the tab at the hotel in Spain while negotiating Yeager's return to England, so Chuck had been able to eat and drink to his heart's content.

After Chuck returned from Spain, he roomed with Bud Anderson. Anderson had just returned from leave and signed up for a second tour of duty. Both men were excellent fighter pilots, skillful and aggressive in combat. The friendship they formed during World War II would last their entire lives.

Once back in England, however, Chuck had to face the idea of never flying in combat again. He was scheduled to fly to New York on June 25, 1944. Although the thought of going home to marry Glennis was appealing, the spirit of pioneer adventure was about to take hold of him once again.

It was standard procedure to send any pilot home once he had been shot down over enemy lines. This was done to protect the identities and locations of the men and women of the Maquis. The Germans knew which pilots had been shot down, and wouldn't think twice about torturing captured pilots to get information about the Maquis.

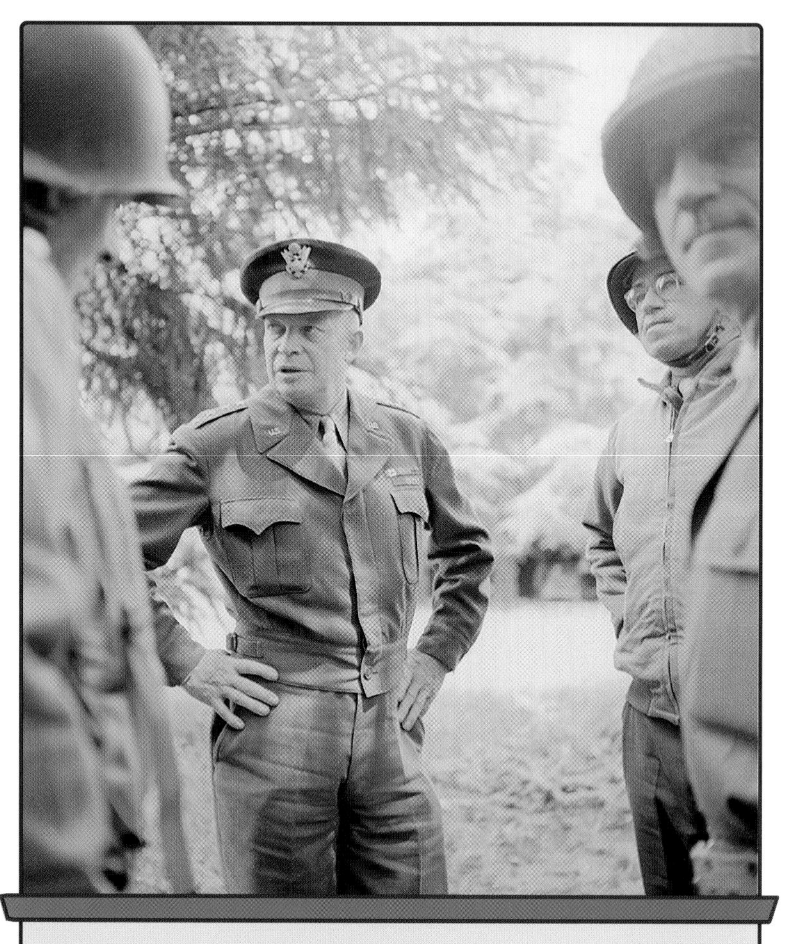

General Dwight D. Eisenhower went to bat for Chuck with the War Department to get him reinstated as a combat pilot. The standard procedure was to send a pilot back to the United States after he had been shot down behind enemy lines, but Eisenhower recognized that Chuck's flying skills were too valuable to waste.

Still, Yeager didn't care. He hadn't spent all that time training to become a fighter pilot to leave the war after completing only 8 missions. He had been taught by his mother and father to finish whatever job he started. Chuck Yeager wasn't done fighting Germans. The young fighter pilot argued his way up through the ranks. Officer after officer told him there was nothing that they could do. Most expressed the desire to help him, since he was, after all, the first evader to make it back to England. Still, he heard time and time again that rules were rules.

On June 12, 1944, Chuck and another evader named Fred Glover met with General Eisenhower. Glover had been working his way through all available channels trying to avoid being sent home, too. This was the last time either Chuck or Glover would have to argue their cases. Eisenhower told the two men that he would have to contact the War Department, but he would see what he could do.

Sometime later, Chuck got the news he was waiting to hear: the War Department had decided to leave the matter up to General Eisenhower. General Eisenhower sent word to Chuck. The fighter pilot would be allowed to fly combat missions again. Chuck was being allowed to stay and fight again with the 363rd.

On October 12, 1944, Chuck Yeager became an ace pilot with five confirmed victories. He was leading a group of fighter planes over Bremen as they escorted some bomber planes on a mission. The young leader set two squadrons along the B-24s to guard them and then flew ahead with his own squadron to scout the skies in front of them. Chuck's squadron was flying over Steinhuder Lake when he noticed something in the air about fifty miles away. As he continued to fly towards the airborne objects, he was able to see what they were—twenty-two German fighters headed in their direction!

The German Me-109s were circling about in the sky, waiting for the American B-24s. They didn't even notice Chuck and his squadron fast approaching in their Mustangs. Chuck moved in toward their tail end. The German pilot saw him and veered to the left, taking out his own wingman. As the planes collided, the two German pilots were forced to parachute out of them. Chuck had scored two victories without even firing one shot!

Next, Chuck destroyed another German fighter from approximately six hundred yards away. As he counted his third victory of the day, a German pilot crept up behind him. Quickly, Chuck pulled back on the throttle and changed direction.

In a testament to his skill as a pilot and aggressive fighting spirit, Chuck pulled his plane right up underneath that German's Me-109. He was now a mere fifty feet below the German fighter pilot. That was the end for that pilot—Chuck opened fire and tallied up his fourth victory of the day.

The fifth victory occurred some moments later. Yeager went into a steep dive, and a German pilot followed him. It was an airplane game of chicken of sorts, better known to pilots as a "dogfight." Chuck pulled up and out in time to avoid the ground, but the German pilot did not.

General Eisenhower would never have to regret his decision to reinstate Chuck Yeager into military combat. The military newspaper of the day, *The Stars and Stripes*, actually ran a headline attesting to Eisenhower's wisdom in reinstating Chuck into combat. The headline read:

FIVE KILLS VINDICATE IKE'S DECISION

Chuck flew 56 more combat missions during World War II. He was credited with shooting down 11 enemy planes. Between July and October of 1944, Chuck was promoted from second lieutenant to captain.

On January 15, 1945, Bud Anderson and Chuck Yeager flew their last mission together. Shortly thereafter, the two fighter pilots flew back to the United States together. Chuck spent one night at the home of Bud Anderson's parents. The following day, February 13, 1945, he celebrated his twenty-second birthday. Bud's mom baked him a cake. But it wasn't birthday cake that had brought Chuck Yeager to California instead of West Virginia on his flight back to the United States. Chuck was on his way to see Glennis. It had been too long since he'd last seen the real Glamorous Glennis, and he was ready to make her his wife.

Chuck showed up at Glennis's door and told her to pack her

A photographer snapped this picture of Chuck in England, just as he stepped out of his P-51 Mustang after shooting down five German planes in one mission.

Chuck returned to the United States, and to Glennis, after shooting down 11 German planes as a member of the Eighth Air Force in Europe. Chuck and Glennis were married, and she was soon pregnant with their first child.

bags, it was time for her to meet his parents. The two boarded a train for West Virginia and headed to Hamlin. They arrived to find a hero's welcome awaiting Chuck.

Glennis and Chuck traveled to Huntington, West Virginia to pick out their wedding rings. Glennis's wedding dress was purchased at the same time. Susie Mae and Pansy Yeager helped Glennis shop for her dress. The family held the wedding in the

Yeagers' living room. Chuck asked J.D. Smith, a local attorney and special friend of his, to give Glennis away. The wedding was held on February 26, 1945.

The young newlyweds spent their honeymoon in Del Mar, California, at an air corps rest and relaxation center. There was another special young couple honeymooning at Del Mar—Bud and Eleanor Anderson. Chuck was surprised and delighted to see his good friend Bud and to meet his new wife.

After two weeks, Glennis headed back to Oroville to pack up her things. Chuck and the Andersons headed off to Texas. The men were to report to Perrin Field. Glennis would catch up with them in Texas. At Perrin Field, Bud and Chuck served as flight instructors, but neither man was cut out for such boring duty. In the air together, the two men couldn't help but stage mock dogfights. According to Glennis Yeager, they often scared new recruits that were flying with them so badly that the young men passed out.

About a month after the two couples arrived at Perrin Field, Eleanor and Glennis were pregnant. Glennis was happy, but a bit nervous about the timing. After all, they had just gotten married.

Chuck and Bud were far from happy at Perrin Field. Their wives were suffering from morning sickness, their jobs were boring to them, and they were not well liked by many of the older officers who resented the two young hotshot fighter pilots who had climbed the ranks so quickly during World War II.

Chuck finally caught a break, however. A new regulation was announced, which allowed anyone who had been a prisoner of war or an evader to choose a duty at the base of their choice. Chuck found the base closest to Hamlin, at Wright Field in Dayton, Ohio. The Yeagers were moving, but Bud and Eleanor, regretfully, would have to stay in Texas.

Breaking the Sound Barrier and Beyond

Chuck Yeager reported to Wright Field in Dayton, Ohio, in July of 1945. Glennis stayed in Hamlin with his parents so that she would have the love and support of her in-laws when Chuck's flying took him away from home.

Chuck was assigned duty as an assistant maintenance officer to the fighter test section of the flight test division. He had walked onto an airbase that was right at the center of flight history. Two weeks after his arrival, Chuck Yeager was flying one of the first functioning American jet fighters.

Chuck used his free time to fly as many different airplanes as Wright Field's hangars held. It was a veritable smorgasbord for the eager flyboy. Wright Field held many captured Japanese and German planes, as well as numerous American planes. Chuck did his best to fly them all.

For fun, Chuck would "attack" the test pilots from his base. He loved forcing them into dogfights. Better still, he loved coming out on top in these dogfights. With his knowledge of mechanics, great vision, and flying skills honed over Germany, he was far superior in a dogfight situation than were any of Wright Field's test pilots.

Some of the test pilots would get angry with Chuck. Others amicably put up with his antics. Some even admired his abilities, although that felt he could be quite a pest at times.

Chuck performed maintenance on the P-80 Shooting Star under the hot sun of the Mojave Desert near Muroc Air Base. Chuck had to fly each plane after repairing it, which meant that he spent more time in the Shooting Stars than most of the test pilots.

The mechanically inclined pilot with the eyes of a hawk and nerves of steel soon caught the attention of Colonel Albert G. Boyd. Colonel Boyd was the head of the flight test division. Thanks to him, Chuck soon found himself seated in the cockpit of a Lockheed P-80 Shooting Star, flying from Muroc Air Base back to Wright Field.

It all happened when Chuck accompanied Colonel Boyd and a group of fighter test pilots to Muroc Air Base. The group was to perform some service tests on the Shooting Star out in the Mojave Desert. Yeager was to serve as the maintenance officer for the group. The desert was hot and the planes were in constant need of repair. As he had to fly each plane after servicing it to check it out, Chuck was getting more fly time in the Shooting Stars than were the fighter test pilots. Colonel Boyd watched the maintenance officer closely.

When their testing period was over, the colonel ordered all but one of the planes to be returned to the Lockheed factory. Then he ordered Chuck to fly the remaining Shooting Star back to Wright Field. This angered the flight section's major, who felt a test pilot should be flying the plane back to Ohio.

The colonel stuck to his guns, however. Yeager climbed into the Shooting Star and pointed her toward Dayton. He made it back safe and sound, too.

In the fall of 1945, Bob Hoover and Chuck Yeager began staging air shows. The two men had forged a great friendship at Wright Field, since both men had the shared experience of being combat pilots in World War II. Now, the nation was crying out for air shows and the test pilots at Wright Field felt that such a duty was beneath them. Hoover and Chuck jumped at the chance. Flying Shooting Stars and being able to do whatever tricks they could accomplish? What could be better? Together the two men traveled the country, buzzing small towns and flying as fast or low as they possibly could.

In November of 1945, after watching Chuck perform in an air show at Wright Field, Colonel Boyd asked him if he would like to become a test pilot. By January of 1946, both Chuck and Hoover were sitting in class together. The two men were officially admitted as students to the test-pilot school.

Yeager credits another student, Jack Ridley, with helping him get through the tough mathematics classes. Jack had studied at Caltech. Always willing to take time out to explain a problem to Chuck, Jack would become another of Yeager's nearest and dearest friends.

Almost immediately after Chuck graduated from test-pilot school, Colonel Boyd told him that he was under consideration for a very special duty. Chuck Yeager was in the running for the job of flying the X-1. If he was chosen for the job, it meant he would be given a chance to break the sound barrier and go down in history as the first pilot to go faster than the speed of sound!

Colonel Boyd asked Chuck who the pilot thought would make a good backup crew for such a test mission. Chuck knew exactly who he'd choose: Bob Hoover as a backup pilot and Jack Ridley as the flight engineer. Colonel Boyd agreed that all three men were worthy of consideration for this important mission. Shortly thereafter, the three men were on their way to Buffalo, New York.

In Buffalo, they toured the Bell Aircraft Corporation Plant. They were briefed on the ins and outs of the X-1. They were shown Bell Aircraft's laboratory. Then, they were allowed to actually check out the X-1. The men were nervous and excited. Not one of them knew who would be flying the X-1 yet, and each wanted a shot at the job. Each of them loved airplanes. Just seeing the X-1 would be the experience of a lifetime for most airplane lovers, but these three guys knew one of them would soon actually be flying it. It was a heady time.

The X-1 was the most impressive airplane any of the three men had ever seen. Its slender wings were made to cut through the air like knives, yet it was built tough enough to withstand the force of 18 Gs. Inside the X-1, the men marveled at the

When Chuck graduated from test-pilot school, Colonel Boyd informed him that he was being considered for a special duty: flying the X-1 in an attempt to break the sound barrier. Instead of taking off from the ground, the X-1 (shown in the foreground of this picture) was launched in midair from a Boeing B-29.

X-1's dozen or so fuel containers. Not only was it carrying enough fuel to create one heck of a bomb, but it entered the sky like a bomb, too. Instead of taking off from the ground like other airplanes, the X-1 was dropped like a bomb from the belly of a B-29 at an altitude of 25,000 feet.

Colonel Boyd soon met with Chuck and asked him what he thought of the X-1. The excited Yeager told him in no uncertain terms that it was the most impressive airplane he had ever seen. Then, to Chuck's amazement and delight, Colonel Boyd asked him if he'd like to fly that impressive plane. Chuck quickly responded yes, and by early July of 1947, the pilot was sent to the Mojave Desert to start practicing and working toward completing the flight of a lifetime.

Time passed. The miles between Glennis and Chuck were just too many. Glennis decided to join him at Muroc. To do so, she would have to leave their young baby, Mickey, with her in-laws for a while and travel with their two-year-old son, Donald, from West Virginia to California. It was a difficult decision for the young wife and mother to make. Still, she and Chuck needed to be together.

Glennis was very touched when Chuck took her to see the X-1. As he had with other planes he had flown, Chuck had named the X-1, *Glamorous Glennis.* The name was written on the nose of the bright orange X-1 for all the world to see.

Shortly afterwards, when Bob Hoover flew back east to get married, Chuck accompanied him. Hoover went to Dayton and was married on September 17, 1947. That very same day, Yeager had picked up the baby from his folks and was headed back to California in the young family's car. Yeager picked up Hoover and his new bride in Dayton and the unlikely foursome made the cross-country trip back to Muroc together.

On October 14, 1947, Chuck Yeager climbed into the X-1 and prepared to take his ninth flight in the experimental craft. So far, he had not been successful at breaking the sound barrier. Shortly beforehand, however, he had succeeded in breaking two of his ribs.

Glennis and Chuck had gone for dinner at a dude ranch known as Pancho's. After dinner, the couple had decided to go for a horseback ride. The young couple rode out into the moonless night, enjoying the ride and each other's company. When it was time to turn back, they decided to race back to the ranch.

Galloping into the ranch, neither Chuck nor his horse saw the gate in front of them until it was too late. Both horse and rider smashed into the gate and Chuck was thrown from his mount. As he struggled to get back on his feet, it became apparent to both him and Glennis that he had broken a rib or two.

Glennis wanted him to see a military doctor. Chuck refused, knowing a military doctor would ground him from flying the X-1 until he healed up completely. Glennis convinced him to at least see a doctor in a neighboring town and the doctor confirmed their suspicions. Chuck had two broken ribs. He taped Chuck's ribs for him and sent him home. There wasn't much more that could be done for cracked or broken ribs.

Chuck met with Jack Ridley to assess the situation. Chuck thought he could fly, but wanted to make sure there wouldn't be any major problems due to his damaged bones. He and Ridley set out to find out if it was safe for Chuck to fly or not. As it turned out, the biggest problem Chuck faced was being able to be mobile enough to lock the X-1's cockpit door. The two men wracked their brains for a solution to the problem and sure enough, they came up with one. Chuck would just have to use a section of broomstick to lock the door. After a few practice runs, Chuck got it down pat. By using the piece of broomstick, he could, indeed, manage to lock the cockpit door.

On October 14, 1947, struggling with two broken ribs but armed with a long section of broomstick, Chuck Yeager took to the skies for his ninth flight in the X-1. Bob Cardenas was flying the mother B-29. At 20,000 feet, he asked if Chuck was ready to go. Chuck gave him a thumbs-up and Cardenas dropped the X-1.

At first, the X-1 started to stall. Chuck never panicked. He wrestled the control panel and brought the X-1's nose down. He was flying it again. He began firing off the rocket chambers.

By the time the X-1 reached 40,000 feet, the plane was still gaining altitude. The X-1's speed was Mach 0.92. Chuck decided to go for it. He had plenty of fuel. After the plane leveled off at an altitude of 42,000 feet, and he had shut down two of the rocket chambers so that he could check his systems, he switched on the third rocket chamber.

The plane's Mach needle hit 0.96. It started to shake a bit. Suddenly, it hit 0.965. Chuck was amazed as he watched it top out. He was flying faster than the speed of sound. The machmeter was tuned to register speed up to Mach 1.0, but the needle was buried at the top of the scale. Chuck knew he was flying faster than Mach 1!

Moments later, he radioed Jack Ridley to report that the machmeter was topped out. As he was doing so, a NACA tracking team was also calling in to report that they had heard a sound like thunder. That sound turned out to be Chuck Yeager's first sonic boom. Chuck's life didn't change much after he broke the sound barrier. Fame and fortune were not immediate. They were, in fact, nonexistent at first. He was still basically

The Bell X-1

The Bell X-1 was built by Bell Aircraft Corporation under the direct supervision of National Advisory Committee for Aeronautics (NACA) and the United States Army Air Force. Built with breaking the sound barrier as its ultimate goal, the X-1 was quite a unique aircraft. The airplane was shaped like a bullet with wings that were fashioned to slice through the atmosphere like two razors.

It was equipped with an XLR-11 engine. This four chamber rocket was nicknamed, "Black Betty." "Black Betty" was fueled by a highly explosive combination of liquid oxygen and dilute ethyl alcohol.

The X-1's wingspan was 28 feet. It was approximately 30 feet in length and 11 feet tall. Empty, the aircraft weighed 7,000 lbs. Its gross weight was 12,250 lbs.

The Bell X-1 was originally designed for standard land takeoffs, but did not generally take advantage of this design. Instead, in most cases, the Bell X-1s were air-launched. This meant they were dropped into the sky by either a Boeing B-29 or a B-50 Superfortress aircraft.

One notable exception to this rule was the Bell X-1, named *Glamorous Glennis.* Despite the danger associated with land takeoffs for the X-1, the Bell X-1 Chuck Yeager flew was once launched from the ground in a successful attempt to break the sound barrier.

The X-1 was originally called the XS-1, which was an abbreviation of "Experimental Supersonic." Three XS-1s were built by Bell Aircraft Corporation of Buffalo, New York. As a result of the success of the XS-1, United States Air Force test pilot Chuck Yeager, NACA scientist John Stack, and Bell Aircraft President Lawrence D. Bell, were awarded the Robert J. Collier trophy in 1947.

just another test pilot. Sure, he'd received the respect and admiration of his peers, but when it came right down to it, he was just a test pilot doing his job. Duty was important to Chuck, and flying was his duty.

The Army did not want anyone to know that Chuck had broken the sound barrier. In fact, they closed ranks and tightened security. Chuck was not to tell anyone what he had accomplished. The guys from the base at Muroc who did know got together and celebrated with him over drinks at the famous "Fly-Inn" at Pancho's ranch. Other than that, the whole affair was kept secret at first.

A few weeks later, on October 27, 1947, Chuck climbed back into the X-1 for another test flight. He was healing up nicely and no longer needed his broomstick to lock the cockpit door. His flight that day would prove to be extremely exciting, to say the least. The B-29 dropped Chuck from its bomb bay and to his dismay, nothing happened. Or rather, gravity happened, but not much of anything else. The X-1's main battery switch was out. Yeager was falling toward the ground and had to think fast.

Chuck credits the ingenuity of an engineer by the name of Dick Frost for saving his life that day. Dick was well-known for constantly coming up with worst-case scenarios and trying to solve them. He had wondered one day what would happen if the battery was not working when they dropped the X-1. Therefore, using a relatively inexpensive valve connected to a bottle of nitrogen gas, the engineer carefully fashioned a manual means for the pilot to slowly blow out the X-1's fuel in case of a battery failure.

That's exactly what Chuck did on October 27th. He level-headedly resorted to Dick Frost's fail-safe valve and began dumping fuel. The experienced pilot knew he was in a seriously dangerous situation. If he didn't get rid of all or most of his fuel, he was going to hit the ground hard, and if that didn't kill him, the resulting explosion surely would.

Miraculously, Chuck was able to dump his fuel. He then guided the X-1 onto the dry lakebed for a bumpy, but quite impressive landing. Fortunately, thanks to his ability to maintain his composure and the work of Dick Frost, Chuck would live to fly another day.

In December of 1947, *Aviation News* announced that the sound barrier had been broken. The air force would not confirm or deny their story. Finally, in June of 1948, the air force formally announced the news that Chuck Yeager had broken the sound barrier. Shortly thereafter, Chuck was awarded the MacKay Trophy by the United States Chief of Staff General Vandenberg in Washington, D.C. The MacKay Trophy was established in 1911 by Clarence H. MacKay, head of the Postal Telegraph-Commercial Cable Companies. It is awarded annually by the U.S. Air Force. The trophy is given to the air force person or persons responsible for the most meritorious flight of the year.

Captain Charles E. Yeager, along with John Stack and Lawrence D. Bell, were awarded the Collier Trophy. Chuck received the Collier Trophy from President Truman. The award ceremony was held at the White House. The Collier Trophy was established in 1911 by Robert J. Collier. Collier was a publisher and one of the first presidents of the Aero Club of America. The trophy is administered by the National Aeronautic Association of the United States of America. The Collier Trophy is awarded on a yearly basis for "the greatest achievement in America, with respect to improving the performance, efficiency, and safety of air or space vehicles, the value of which has been thoroughly demonstrated by actual use during the preceding year."

Chuck was now a national celebrity and treasure. Still, he couldn't say much when requested to speak before admiring groups of fans. Most of the details concerning his supersonic flight and the X-1 were still classified!

On January 5, 1949, Chuck, Jack Ridley, and a small flight crew accomplished another amazing feat. Together, they figured out a way to allow Chuck to fly the X-1 from a land takeoff and still manage to break the sound barrier. The navy had been attempting to do this with their rocket-powered Skystreak, but Chuck, Ridley, and crew beat them to it. The air force swelled with pride. Yeager and friends had done it again.

In the summer of 1950, *Glamorous Glennis* was sent to the Smithsonian Institute. Jack Ridley flew it to the museum with Chuck. Chuck had flown the plane he named after his wife, but often still referred to as the "orange beast," on thirty-three test flights. He had achieved a speed of 1.45 Mach, or 957 mph, in the plane. Now, it belonged to the annals of history. The X-1 was retired.

Captain Chuck Yeager still had work to do, however. Even if the X-1 was retired, he wasn't. On December 12, 1953 at Edwards Air Force Base in California, Chuck once more took to the skies in an experimental aircraft. This time it was in the Bell X-1A. The Bell X-1A was comparable to the Bell X-1. However, it had turbo-driven fuel pumps rather than a pressurized nitrogen system. It also had a redesigned cockpit canopy, a longer fuselage, and greater fuel capacity than the Bell X-1.

The craft was to be carried into the skies by a B-29. This was so that its pilot was able to reserve all of its rocket fuel for use in achieving a supersonic speed. The plane was only 31 feet long, but it was one of the sturdiest and most aerodynamic planes ever made at that time.

Chuck and his crew moved the X-1A into position beneath the B-29. It was locked into place. The crew pumped liquid oxygen and a mixture of water and alcohol into it. All said, when these fluids were combined, the plane's pilot would have 30,000 horsepower at his disposal.

Chuck and the B-29 crew were dressed in high altitude suits. They climbed aboard the B-29. It was time to try to push Chuck all the way to Mach 2 in the X-1A. A chase plane followed as the B-29 took off into the sky.

The X-lA was dropped and Chuck cued the first rocket chamber. The plane sped up quickly. It immediately pulled far ahead of the chase plane and broke Mach 1 with little or no difficulty. Chuck was flying faster than the speed of sound, once again. He took the X-1A up to an elevation of 70,000 feet and accelerated the plane to a speed of over 1,600 miles per hour, or Mach 2.5. The chase plane was far, far behind him.

Suddenly, the nose of the plane began to pull to the left. One of the plane's wings came up, and Chuck and the X-1A began to roll over. Chuck was experiencing what became known as an inertia coupling phenomenon. The aerodynamics experts at Bell had warned that the X-1A might perform that way at speeds faster than Mach 2.4, and they had been right. Somehow, Chuck kept his head and managed to pull out of the spin at 25,000 feet. Bruised and battered from the plane's rolling and spinning, Chuck landed the X-1A on the lakebed. He was visibly shaken, but had once again shattered another record. He would later learn that he had dropped an amazing 51,000 feet in 51 seconds.

Chuck was in the spotlight once again. President Eisenhower acknowledged his flying talents by personally awarding him the Harmon International Trophy. Named for Clifford B. Harmon, a wealthy sportsman and aviator, three Harmon Trophies are awarded each year. These are given to the world's greatest aviator, aviatrix, and aeronaut.

A North Korean pilot, Lieutenant Kim Sok Ho, would soon decide upon a course of action that would directly influence Yeager's career as a test pilot. Ho defected in his plane and basically sold it to the United States government for a cool $100,000—quite a bit of money during the early 1950s. The U.S. government wanted only the best test pilots to fly and review this MiG-15.

In February of 1954, Chuck was assigned a short-term duty at Kadena Air Force Base in Okinawa, Japan, to test the Russian

Bruised and shaken, Chuck Yeager climbs from the cockpit of his X1-A after plunging more than 51,000 feet in less than a minute. One of Chuck's greatest strengths as a pilot was his ability to stay focused under pressure.

MiG-15. The MiG-15s were being used against American pilots and their Sabres over the skies of Korea. Yeager and another test pilot, Tom Collins, were assigned to figure out the MiG-15. It was their job to learn all about it and then decide just how an American pilot should go about beating it in a dogfight.

For a week, the two men secretly flew test flights over Japan, testing the MiG-15's limits.

When their job was done, Yeager received a phone call—his years as a test pilot had come to an end. He was then offered a choice: he could accept desk duty at Edwards or he could accept command of the 417th Fighter-Bomb Squadron in Germany.

Chuck had spent over nine years of his life testing the limits of supersonic flight. Figuring that even with his skill and commitment to excellence, he had pushed the odds plenty as a test pilot, he decided it was indeed time for a change.

He accepted the offer to assume command duty with the 417th Fighter-Bomber Squadron in Germany. Glennis was excited about traveling to Germany. It was time to leave the desert, time to say farewell for now to Edwards Air Force Base. Their friends hosted a going away party for them at Pancho's Ranch and with that, Chuck and Glennis were off to Europe.

In October of 1954, with Glennis and his children by his side, Chuck assumed command of the 417th Fighter Squadron in Germany. In September of 1957, after three years in Europe with the 417th, Chuck, Glennis and their children returned to the United States. At that time, he served as commander of the 1st Fighter Squadron at George Air Force Base in California.

In 1959, Chuck traveled to Russia with a woman named Jackie Cochran. Jackie was an accomplished pilot who had set a speed record back in May of 1953 flying a Canadian-built Sabre. Chuck had been her chase pilot, as well as her mentor.

Not only had Jackie been a dear friend of the famous Amelia Earhart, but she was also beloved by many among the nation's top brass. Her husband was a wealthy and quite powerful industrialist named Floyd Odlum. Floyd and Jackie and Chuck and Glennis became close friends soon after they first met in the late 1940s.

Now Jackie was traveling to Russia and she had requested that Chuck be allowed to accompany her. The Air Force Chief

President Dwight D. Eisenhower awarded the Harmon Trophy to Chuck Yeager and Jackie Cochran in 1954 for their achievements as pilots. Chuck was the first man, and Jackie the first woman, to break the sound barrier.

of Staff, General Tommy White, was a close friend of Jackie's. White and the U.S. Air Force saw this as a great opportunity for Chuck to be their eyes and ears within the borders of Russia.

Chuck spent about two months overseas with Jackie Cochran. They met with Russian diplomats, fighter pilots, and military chiefs. At first, they were careful to downplay Chuck's identity. They wanted the Russians to think that he was just a civilian copilot along for the ride with Jackie.

At a formal dinner, however, a Russian diplomat overheard someone refer to Chuck as "Mr. Yeager." He immediately questioned Chuck as to whether or not he was really the great

American test pilot. Honest to a fault, Chuck answered that he was indeed.

A few days later, Andre Tupolev, a brilliant Russian aircraft engineer, arranged to meet privately with Chuck. The two men exchanged pleasantries and verbally sparred, each trying to get information from the other. Still, the meeting was amicable and the two parted on good terms. Chuck was certain that the two large, quiet men who had accompanied Tupolev had been recording their conversation. He was also sure that he had not divulged any information that the Russians didn't already have.

After two months abroad playing spy with Jackie Cochran, Chuck was ready to return home. He had had enough of Russia and was ready to move on to other things. His next big adventure was to be a scholastic endeavor. Chuck Yeager was soon to be enrolled in the Air War College—a school designed to educate senior officers to lead at the highest levels of the air force and space programs.

Pilots Fly, Astronauts Ride

During the time Chuck was enrolled in the Air War College in Alabama, Glennis stayed behind in Victorville, California, where their children were in school. Chuck spent most weekends in Victorville with Glennis and the kids, and most weekdays away at the Air War College.

As the months passed, Chuck spent much of his time studying. He was also flying any and every available airplane every chance he got. He was promoted to colonel during this time, too.

Halfway through the school year, Jackie Cochran appealed to General Tommy White to allow her to take Chuck to Spain. She was meeting with the Russians to discuss the rules of the Sporting Committee. This group was part of the Fédération Aéronautique Internationale (FAI)—the world governing body for air sports—and endorsed aviation records for worldwide recognition. Jackie believed that Chuck's fame among the Russians would help her to successfully negotiate with them.

The educators at the Air War College were not pleased with Jackie's request to pull Chuck from his studies. In fact, they effectively told Jackie and General White that there was no way he could leave. Still, she kept at it, and an angry General White wrote out orders for Chuck to accompany her to Spain.

Jackie Cochran wanted Chuck to accompany her on a trip to Spain to negotiate the rules for the FAI—the world governing body for air sports and world aviation records. She believed she could use Chuck's fame to help her in the negotiations.

General White was not about to let the Air War College dictate protocol to him.

Chuck spent a week in Spain with Jackie and the Russians. During that week, they got the FAI records squared away. An agreement declaring that an altitude of 50 miles would be considered outer space was also reached.

Chuck returned to the Air War College and graduated, and was appointed as the head of the Air Force Aerospace Research Pilot School. The new school was to be the Air Force's training ground for astronauts. Yeager was its chief administrator.

During his years at the school, Chuck was able to accomplish a great deal. The school was home to a revolutionary $6,000,000 space simulator. Students at the school became adept in the use of computers. Chuck even helped to acquire the funds to take three Lockheed Starfighters and turn them into aircraft that would allow student pilots to experience weightlessness.

The school started out with a class of eleven. The first two classes were composed of graduates of the Air Force test-pilot school. After that, the school began running two courses. The first six months was a course in test piloting. The next six months was a course in space training.

Eventually, the school grew large enough to accommodate 26 students. Men from the navy and the marines came to study under Chuck's staff. A few NATO countries even had students apply and gain acceptance into the famous flyer's academy.

Only one event really ever threatened to tarnish Chuck's time at the school. An unfortunate incident, involving an unqualified student, grew into a potential political disaster. In 1961, Bobby Kennedy made it known that he wanted a African-American man in space. The problem began when only one African-American pilot applied to the school and he didn't make the grade.

The pilot was actually 26th on the list. At that time in

U.S. Attorney General Robert Kennedy pressured Chuck to admit an African-American student to the U.S. Air Force Aerospace Research Pilot School. Chuck did as he was told, but was charged with discrimination when the pilot was not chosen by NASA for the space program.

the school's history, only eleven pilots were being accepted into the school. The school had already published the list of the top fifteen pilots when Chief of Staff, General Curtis LeMay, basically ordered Chuck to get an African-American student into the school.

Chuck was between a rock and a hard place. He bargained

with LeMay. After securing enough additional funding to accommodate sixteen students, Chuck added the African-American pilot's name to the bottom of the published fifteen names. Chuck's problems, however, had just begun.

The student was trying, but not succeeding academically. The school supplied him with tutors to help. His flying was not up to par with the other students' skills either. Yeager was relieved when, at graduation time, the problematic student received his diploma. To the chagrin of the White House, and probably to Bobby Kennedy in particular, the African-American pilot was not chosen by NASA to train for their space program.

The student charged Colonel Yeager with discrimination. Chuck was furious. If anything, he had bent over backwards to help this young man make it through the school against his own better judgment. Chuck did request that the young pilot be court-martialed for insubordination. His request was denied, however. It seemed that Chuck's superiors just wanted the whole mess to go away.

In 1963, Chuck would be faced with a different sort of mess. And this one would not go away anywhere nearly as easily or as painlessly as the whole discrimination affair had gone away. In fact, this mess was quite time consuming and would prove to be excruciatingly painful for Chuck.

In an interview copyrighted by the American Academy of Achievement, Chuck described the incident in these words, "When I was commandant of the astronaut school, we had to train the guys in a simulated space environment. We took three F-104As, which was a Mach-2 airplane, and we put a hydrogen peroxide rocket engine in the tail, above the normal jet engine [which] gave us an additional 6000 pounds of thrust. And with this aircraft, we also added 24 inches to the wingtip and two hydrogen peroxide thrusters, one out the top of each wing tip and one out the bottom. That's for roll control above the atmosphere. We extended the nose of the airplane out and put thrusters in the top and

A Brief Flight Glossary

Ailerons—Control surfaces found on the wing of the airplane, often near the tips. Ailerons control the airplane around the roll axis. As one aileron goes up, the other goes down. This way, as one aileron forces air to push its side of the wing down, the plane rolls in that direction. To roll right, the pilot must raise the right aileron, pushing the left aileron down.

Airplane Axis—The line around which a plane rotates.

Drag—The air resistance to forward motion.

Elevator—A device used for pitch control that makes the airplane raise or lower its nose. This results in a climbing or diving response.

Horizontal Stabilizer—The horizontal tail surface, which provides the airplane with pitch stability.

Intake—An air inlet.

Nose—The front of a plane's fuselage.

Pitch—The angle from the front to back of the plane. The pitch tells whether the nose of the plane is pointing high or low in relation to the ground. Pitch is controlled by the elevator(s).

Roll Axis—Controlled by the ailerons. Dropping either wingtip of an airplane is the start of its roll movement. The roll axis is used to bank or turn the airplane.

Roll—The pilot points the nose of the airplane in one direction and rolls the plane over onto its back. The pilot then brings the plane back to an upright position to complete the roll.

Rudder—The moveable element of the vertical tail surface. The rudder directs the airplane around the yaw axis. (see **Yaw** and **Yaw Axis**)

Thrust—The forward force provided by the airplane's engine. Thrust moves the airplane forward.

Yaw—Movement of the airplane's nose to the left or to the right is its yaw. Yaw is controlled by the rudder.

Yaw Axis—The airplane axis controlled by the rudder.

bottom and each side for pitch control and yaw control of the airplane.

"We knew the 104 had a pitch-up problem, meaning when the airplane stalled, it pitched up. I was the first military pilot to fly the 104, on August 3, 1954. I was the test pilot on that airplane, so I knew it intimately. I spun the airplane a lot, and stalled it. I knew we had this problem."

Chuck and his team ran a series of test flights with Chuck as the pilot. Their goal was to work out all the problems they were experiencing with the plane before exposing student test pilots to any unnecessary dangers. Chuck flew the plane more than 40 times, testing different solutions to different problems.

Speaking about performing these tests, Chuck told an interviewer, "We thought we would run one more. I flew a flight in the morning, with a pressure suit on, I think at 108,000 feet, and we measured the rotation. Then I landed and wanted to make another flight after lunch. I didn't get out of my pressure suit because if you get out of it, it's wet and you can't get back in. I made another flight at about 1:30 in the afternoon, at 104,000 feet. For some reason, we had dual thrusters on the bottom of the nose and dual thrusters on the top. We don't know, we may have had one thruster fail, but at 104,000 feet, when I came into the atmosphere at a 50° angle of attack, I couldn't get the nose down on the airplane. You've already shut your engine down, and it gradually is slowing down. But the engine is still turning over, giving you hydraulic pressure, which runs the horizontal stabilizer for pitch control, the ailerons, and the rudder.

"What happened on previous flights, when you re-enter and force the nose down with the hydrogen peroxide thrusters, the altitude controllers, then you come back into the atmosphere nose first. Then you start getting air through the intake ducts of your airplane, that keeps your engine windmilling, you bring the airplane on down to about 40,000 feet, level out, hit the igniter and then come out of idle, out of stop cock with your throttle into idle. That gives you fuel and you start you engine up again. But if it doesn't work, you go on down, dead stick into Rogers Dry Lake, which I did three or four times.

"What happened on this flight was that when the airplane came into the atmosphere, at about a 50° angle of attack, I couldn't get the nose down. The airplane pitched up and went into a flat spin. Now airplane is in a flat spin and, because there is no air going through the intake ducts, the engine stops. When that stops, then you no longer have hydraulic pressure to run the horizontal stabilizer, the aileron or the rudder. So you are in a no-win situation. That's exactly what it is. You sit there. But you have one other alternative, that's eject. I also had a drag chute on the airplane that we use for landing. The airplane was in a very flat, slow spin. I had my pressure suit on and it was inflated. I sat there and watched. I was talking to Bud Anderson who was chasing me in a T-33. He was down, way down though, looking at me coming," Chuck continued.

Chuck realized he could not pull the airplane out of its spin. It was time to make some very serious decisions. He deployed his drag chute, but he was moving at 180 mph. The drag chute was designed to shred at 180 mph, so that in case it ever accidentally deployed, it wouldn't slow you down. The design team would have been proud, as the drag chute was cut off. This didn't help Chuck's plight.

Chuck was sitting in a rocket seat. He waited until he was at about 6,000 feet, and ejected. The rocket seat blew him out and away from the airplane. Chuck described the experience with these words, "I sat and watched the seat go through a sequencing, knowing when it was going to happen. Finally the lap belt popped open, and there is a butt kicker that kicks you out of the seat. I felt that go and also my cable cutters cut my leg restrainer cable from me [and] I fell through.

Drag chutes on jets like this SR-71 were designed to slow a fast-moving airplane during landing. Chuck tried to pull his airplane out of a spin by deploying a similar drag chute, but it was shredded to pieces because he was traveling too fast.

When this happened, the release on your parachute is armed and as you fall through 1400 feet, the chute opens. Well, I was below 1400 feet, so the chute opened the minute that the release said to open, and it did. The problem was, I didn't have enough velocity through the air, I was just starting to fall again, to pull that quarter bag which is on the canopy of your parachute. The reason that bag is on the canopy is that when you eject at high speeds, four or five hundred miles an hour, it keeps your canopy on the parachute from popping immediately. The little pilot chute on that quarter bag needs about 60 mph to pull it off the quarter bag. I didn't know anything like this was going on, all I know is that I am free falling, my chute has released, but I haven't got a canopy slowing me down because I can feel it flopping in the breeze.

"At about this time, the seat, which kicked me out up here, is also falling and it became entangled in the shroud lines of the parachute. I didn't know this either, but this is the way it happened. Finally I picked up enough speed, 60 or 70 mph, with the canopy up there following, that quarter bag came off, the canopy popped and when it popped, the seat that is entangled in the shroud lines flopped me up like this. The seat hit me in the face piece of my pressure suit. And what hit me was the butt end of the rocket on the seat, which still had glowing propellant burning. When this happened, it popped glowing propellant onto the rubber seals of my pressure suit. You are in 100 percent oxygen, so it ignited and you are feeding 100 percent oxygen. It's like a blow torch.

"Fortunately, when this happened, the visor on my pressure suit was busted and frayed, it cut my eye down and my eye socket filled with blood, so it didn't hurt my eyeball. I got burned pretty bad on my neck and shoulder and it was very difficult to breathe. The only thing I knew, I was stunned from the blow, I knew I had to get the visor up on my pressure suit helmet. There is a button on the right, you push it and then you raise your visor. It's the way you get your visor up on most pressure suits. I knew I had to get it off, get that visor up to shut the oxygen flow from my kit that was in the back of my pressure suit to get all this fire out. So I did that. Then I swung a couple times and hit the ground. I couldn't see too much and I was having trouble breathing because there was a lot of smoke and fire.

"But it worked out, you either do or your don't, and I didn't get killed in the flat. I stood up and Andy buzzed me. Since I had been talking to them on the way down, four minutes from the first spin to impact, they had a helicopter off with a flight surgeon aboard, a doctor at Edwards. He got out there, probably within five minutes of the time I landed, picked me up, gave me a shot of morphine and took me back to the hospital. They worked on me, cut my pressure suit off and that was about it."

What Chuck didn't say in that interview was that he spent a month in the hospital, enduring a painful new skin scraping technique to keep his face from becoming permanently disfigured. His doctor, Dr. Bear, scraped the scabs from his face and neck every four days. Thankfully, the technique, although extremely painful, was extremely successful. Chuck survived first, second, and third degree burns and still managed to look good afterwards. He also walked away from the crash with a new record; he was the first pilot to emergency eject while wearing the full pressure suit used for high altitude flights.

Three years later, in 1966, Chuck was headed to Vietnam. He exchanged his command at the school for a wing command in South East Asia. In a show of support for her husband and his flyboys, Glennis volunteered in the lab at the Clark Air Force Base in the Philippines. For two years, Chuck commanded the 405th. After serving as the 405th's commander, Chuck was sent to command a group of F-4 Phantoms at Seymour Johnson in North Carolina. This group was sent over to South Korea for six months during the Pueblo crisis, which involved the capture of the navy's ship, the USS *Pueblo*, by the North Koreans. Chuck was practical and quite paternal, so he made the most of his situation while stationed in Korea and flew into Vietnam as often as he could. After all, his son, Don, was stationed in Vietnam. What father wouldn't check in on his son, if possible, under such circumstances?

In the autumn of 1968, Chuck and his men were sent back to North Carolina from their station in Korea. He returned to North Carolina with a perfect deployment record. This record did not go unnoticed. He had brought three squadrons of F-4 Phantoms back home intact.

Chuck was proud to lead a flyby—a low-altitude, ceremonial flight—over President Eisenhower's funeral as these military men carried his coffin to its final resting place.

Shortly after his return from Korea, Chuck received a message to telephone his friend, Lieutenant General Gordon Graham. He called Gordie, thinking that he was in trouble with a four-star general by the name of Momyer. Momyer was Chuck's boss, and he and Chuck were far from friendly.

Gordie had good news for Chuck, however. Colonel Chuck Yeager would now be answering to a new title: General Yeager. The excited new general first told his wife, Glennis, the good news and then shared it with his maintenance crews. Just days later, Chuck was leading a flyby in Washington, D.C. The flyby was held in honor of the late President Eisenhower. The funeral was solemn and the weather was bad. Still, the flyby went on without a problem.

Months passed. Glennis and Chuck were off to Germany, once again. This time, Chuck was to serve as the vice commander of the Seventeenth Air Force. The couple spent a year and a half in Germany.

December of 1970 arrived and with it came a new assignment for General Yeager. Air force headquarters was sending him to Pakistan. General Charles E. Yeager would now be the new U.S. Defense Representative to Pakistan. His real mission while in Pakistan was to assist in the training of the Pakistani air force. He was to help them learn how to best use Sidewinder missiles. Eventually, Chuck learned that fellow West Virginian Joe Farland, Ambassador to Pakistan, had requested that General Yeager be given the job of U.S. Defense Representative to Pakistan. So, for the next 18 months, the Yeagers would be living in Pakistan.

In 1973, Chuck was stationed at Norton, California. He was now the Safety Director of the Air Force. Normally, generals are not allowed to fly their own planes. Chuck was not going to stand for such a thing, however. His argument was simple. He did not feel that he could be the Safety Director for the Air Force without safety-testing airplanes himself. The Pentagon gave in to his argument and allowed him to fly. Their only demand was that he have a pilot on board with him whenever he flew.

In 1973, the Aviation Hall of Fame in Dayton, Ohio inducted Chuck into its group of famed aviators. Chuck was now honored amongst the likes of the legendary flight pioneers Wilbur and Orville Wright, as well as famed fighter pilot Eddie Rickenbacker.

In 1975, Chuck decided it was time to retire. Ever the pilot at heart, he agreed to serve as a unpaid consultant for both NASA and the air force. Part of his work for both outfits would be to fly airplanes. That would be pay enough for the airplane-loving retired brigadier general.

Chuck Yeager has been asked by many people whether he

regrets not having been a member of any of the teams of astronauts that went up into space. His answer varies slightly, but always boils down to the same sentiment. Yeager is a pilot. He wants control of his vehicle. So, he tells folks he has no regrets. After all, pilots fly, while astronauts merely ride. And Chuck is all pilot!

"The Right Stuff"

On Wednesday, December 8, 1976, retired Brigadier General Charles E. Yeager was awarded a Special Congressional Silver Medal by Gerald Ford, the President of the United States of America. Jackie Cochran had lobbied steadfastly to see that Chuck received this award. Her efforts had paid off. Unfortunately, she was too ill to attend the award ceremony. Still, she was pleased that Chuck had been honored by the president and a grateful nation.

Chuck's citation reads, "For conspicuous gallantry and total disregard for his personal safety on October 14, 1947 as pilot of the XS-1 research aircraft. On this date, Brigadier General (then Captain) Yeager advanced aerospace science a quantum step by proving that an aircraft could be flown at supersonic speeds. He dispelled for all time the mythical 'sound barrier' and set the stage for unprecedented aviation advancement. Through his selfless dedication to duty and his heroic challenge of the unknown, General Yeager performed inestimable service to the Nation far above and beyond the call of duty and brought great credit upon himself and the United States of America."

A few years later, in 1979, Tom Wolfe's book, *The Right Stuff*, was published. The book detailed the early years of the

President Ronald Reagan appointed Chuck to serve on the National Commission on Space and the commission to investigate the space shuttle *Challenger* accident. Reagan presented Chuck with the Presidential Medal of Freedom for his record-setting achievements as a test pilot.

space program from 1947 through 1963. Chuck is often asked what the right stuff is and whether or not he thinks he has it.

From 1979 through 1983, Glennis's mom lived with Chuck and Glennis. She had suffered a stroke and needed constant care. Chuck and Glennis cared for her until her death in November of 1983.

Hal Needham, director of the movie *Smokey and the Bandit*, knew who had the right stuff when he wanted to test the limits of a rocket-powered car. He called upon Yeager. Together, the men were able to get a car up to the speed of Mach 1. Yeager helped to achieve this feat at a familiar stomping ground: Rogers Dry Lake Bed.

In 1983, the Academy Award-winning film, *The Right Stuff*, was directed by Philip Kaufman. The movie opened with Chuck breaking the sound barrier in the X-1 jet plane. Chuck has a cameo role in the film; he plays a bartender. Sam Shepherd plays Chuck Yeager in the film.

In 1985, Chuck published his autobiography, *Yeager*. The book is co-authored by Leo Janos and became a best-seller. In it, Chuck, his wife, and his closest friends tell the story of his life from birth to 1985. He also celebrated his fortieth wedding anniversary with Glennis on February 25, 1985.

Glennis bravely battled cancer and Chuck stood lovingly beside her through her trials. In his autobiography, he gives her what is to him the greatest compliment he could give to another human being. Speaking about her victory against cancer and about her bravery and toughness during her battle, Chuck remarks that Glennis would have been, "one helluva great pilot."

Chuck continued to serve his nation after retiring from active duty. In 1986, President Ronald Reagan appointed Chuck to serve on the National Commission on Space and the commission to investigate the space shuttle *Challenger* accident in 1986. Who better to get to the bottom of such a national tragedy?

Chuck faced a more personal tragedy in December of 1990. His beloved Glennis passed away. Known for her beauty, Glennis was also a very intelligent woman. Much more than just Chuck's wife, Glennis had also been the CEO of his consulting business, Yeager, Inc.

Chuck was awarded the Elder Statesman of Aviation Award in 1994. As if to prove his worthiness of such an award, at the age of 74, Chuck celebrated his 50th anniversary of breaking the sound barrier by breaking the sound barrier once again! This time, the Brigadier General flew an F-15 fighter to get the job done.

Chuck Yeager, retired brigadier general, is known to many people throughout the world as the best American pilot that ever lived. Famous for being the man who broke the sound barrier, Chuck is much more than just that. He is the epitome of the American dream.

A poor boy from West Virginia, Chuck worked hard to become the best pilot he could possibly be. Through sheer hard work and tenacity, he rose through the ranks to become a brigadier general. He never gave up. Instead, even in the direst of situations—such as being stuck behind enemy lines in World War II or spinning wildly out of control in an experimental aircraft—he always forged ahead.

Chuck has the right stuff, all right. He is indeed a flyer worthy of the fame he has achieved. A humble, honest man, Chuck is the type of hero that all Americans can be proud to claim as one of their own.

Perhaps President George Bush summed up Yeager's character best in a letter he wrote to Chuck commemorating his 50th anniversary of breaking the sound barrier. The president wrote, "If I was asked to choose one word that would define Chuck Yeager, it would be 'service.' Fighter pilot, test pilot, combat commander—you have always valued service to our country above all else."

1923

February 13 Charles E. Yeager was born in Myra, West Virginia.

1939-1940 Attends the Citizens Military Training Camp at Fort Benjamin Harrison, Indiana.

1941

September 12 Enlists as a private in the Army Air Corps.

1942

July Accepted for pilot training under the "Flying Sergeant Program."

1943

March Receives his pilot wings and appointment as a flight officer at Luke Field, Arizona.

1944

March 5 Shot down on his eighth combat mission over German-occupied France.

Summer Returns to his squadron and flies 56 more combat missions, shooting down 11 more German aircraft.

July-October Promoted from second lieutenant to captain.

1945 Attends the instructor pilot course then serves as an instructor pilot at Perrin Field, Texas.

July Goes to Wright Field, Ohio, and participates in various test projects including the P-80 "Shooting Star" and the P-84 Thunder jet.

1946

January Attends the Test Pilot School at Wright Field, Ohio, and in August 1947 was sent to Muroc Air Base, California, as the project officer on the Bell X-1.

1947

October 14 Breaks the sound barrier in the X-1, becoming the world's first supersonic pilot.

1952 Attends the Air Command and Staff College at Maxwell Air Force Base, Alabama.

1953

December Flies the Bell X-1A at 1,650 mph, becoming the first man to fly at Mach 2.5.

1954 Travels to Europe to serve as commander of the 417th Fighter Squadron, at Hahn Air Base, West Germany, and at Toul-Rosieres Air Base, France.

1957 Assigned to the 413th Fighter Wing at George Air Force Base, California.

1958 Becomes commander of the 1st Fighter Squadron, flying new F-100 "Super Sabres."

1961

June Graduates from the Air War College, Maxwell Air Force Base, Alabama.

1962 Becomes commandant of the U.S. Air Force Aerospace Research Pilot School.

1963

December 10 Parachutes to safety during a crash while testing an NF-104 rocket-augmented aerospace trainer.

1966

July Flies 127 missions in South Vietnam as commander of the 405th Fighter Wing at Clark Air Base, Republic of the Philippines.

1968

February Deployed to the Republic of Korea during the USS *Pueblo* crisis.

1969

July Becomes vice commander of Seventh Air Force at Ramstein Air Base, West Germany.

August Promoted to brigadier general.

1971 Becomes U.S. Defense Representative to Pakistan.

1973

March Stationed at the Air Force Inspection and Safety Center, Norton Air Force Base, California, and becomes director in June 1973.

1975

March 1 Retires from active duty in the U.S. Air Force.

1986 Appointed by President Ronald Reagan to serve on the National Commission on Space and the commission to investigate the space shuttle *Challenger* accident.

1994 Awarded Elder Statesman of Aviation Award.

1997 Makes last flight as a military consultant on October 14, 1997, at age 74. This is the 50th anniversary of his sound-barrier-breaking flight in the X-1. Chuck celebrates the occasion by once again breaking the sound barrier in an F-15 fighter. U.S. Postal Service issues special stamp to commemorate the 50th anniversary of supersonic flight.

Famous Firsts in American Aviation

Airborne American—June 24, 1784—Edward Warren of Baltimore, Maryland, age 13, went aloft in a captive balloon built by Peter Carnes, who was either afraid to go up or was too heavy to be lifted.

Glider flight—March 17, 1883—John J. Montgomery began the first of a series of glider flights at Otay Mesa, California.

Parachute jump—January 30, 1887—Thomas E. Baldwin jumped from a balloon in San Francisco, California. It would be 25 years until this feat was tried from an airplane.

Airplane factory—1900—Carl Dryden Browne started a commercial airplane factory in Freedom, Kansas, and built a model but was unable to perfect his aircraft. The factory closed in 1902.

Airplane patent—March 23, 1903—The Wright brothers applied for the first U.S. patent based on their 1902 glider. It was issued on May 22, 1906.

Man-controlled powered flight—December 17, 1903—Orville Wright made a 12-second flight of 120 feet at Kitty Hawk, North Carolina. (Wilbur Wright had tried three days earlier and failed to get airborne; however, he made the second flight this historic day of 850 feet in 69 seconds.)

Fully controllable and maneuverable flight—June 23, 1905—First flight of the Wright Flyer #3 at Huffman Prairie, Dayton, Ohio, in which a fully controllable aircraft was able to turn, bank, and remain aloft for up to 30 minutes.

Distance and duration record—October 5, 1905—Wilbur Wright, in Wright Flier #3, flew for 24.2 miles in 38 minutes and 3 seconds.

Aero exhibition—January 1906—New York Aero Show, in connection with the annual Auto Show.

Air Service—August 1, 1907—The Aeronautical Division of the Signal Corps was formed, and two enlisted men under the command of Captain Charles Chandler were detailed to handle "all matters pertaining to military ballooning, air machines, and all kindred subjects."

Flight in which a motion picture camera was used—April 24, 1908—Wilbur Wright piloted his Flier at Centocelle, Italy, with a cinematographer as passenger.

Passenger flight—May 14, 1908—Wilbur Wright took along Charles Furnas, an employee, in a check flight for delivery of a government airplane.

Military pilot—May 19, 1908—Army Lieutenant Thomas E. Selfridge.

Flying club and civil airport—June 10, 1908—The Aeronautical Society formed in New York City and established Morris Park airfield—the first real airport.

Air ordinances—July 17, 1908—Laws were passed governing local aeronautical activities at Kissimmee, Florida.

Altitude, distance, and duration record—August 8, 1908—Wilbur Wright surpassed existing French flight records for all three categories at Camp d'Auvours, France.

Fatality in a powered airplane—September 17, 1908—Lieutenant Thomas E. Selfridge was killed while riding as a passenger with Orville Wright in a demonstration flight at Ft. Myer, Virginia.

Rotary-wing aircraft—1909—William Purvis and Charles Wilson, railroad mechanics in Goodland, Kansas, quit their jobs to work on a rotary-winged aircraft. The venture failed, but their design is believed to be the first rotary-winged aircraft—a predecessor to the helicopter.

Commercial civil aircraft—January 22, 1909—A "Pusher" built by Glenn H. Curtiss for sale to the Aeronautic Society of New York.

Airplane dealership—June 22, 1909—Wyckoff, Church & Partridge, auto dealers in New York City, acquired the Curtiss line.

Army airplane—August 2, 1909—A Wright Model A was purchased by the army for $25,000, plus $5,000 as a bonus for exceeding required specifications. Delivered to Ft. Myer, Virginia.

Speed record—August 23, 1909—At the world's first major air meet in Rheims, France, Glenn Curtiss became the first American to claim the recognized speed record by flying at 43.385 mph in his biplane.

Monoplane flight—December 9, 1909—Dr. Henry W. Walden. Technically, this was the first monoplane flight, albeit only for about 30 feet. His subsequent flights in August 1910 are more often credited with this record.

Pilot license—1910—Glenn Curtiss was the recipient of license #1. Four more were awarded that year: #2: Frank Lahm; #3: Louis Paulhan; #4: Orville Wright; #5: Wilbur Wright. When licensing first began, licenses were assigned alphabetically.

Commercial flight school—March 19, 1910—Orville Wright opened the first Wright Flying School in Montgomery, Alabama.

Night flight—June 1910—Charles W. Hamilton, over Knoxville, Tennessee.

Mile-high altitude record—July 17, 1910—Walter Brookins was awarded $5000 for climbing 6,234 feet into the sky in his Wright Model A over Atlantic City, New Jersey.

Gun fired from an airplane—August 20, 1910—Two shots were fired from a Curtiss biplane at a ground target with a rifle by Lieutenant Jacob A. Fickel at Sheepshead Bay, New York.

Air-to-ground radio—August 27, 1910—James McCurdy sent and received messages in a Curtiss biplane.

Woman to solo an airplane—September 2, 1910—Blanche Scott; however, since it was never established if her brief flight, measured in seconds, was intentional or accidental (some witnesses claimed it was caused by a gust of wind), Bessica Medlar Raiche is most often credited with the first solo flight by a woman on September 16, 1910.

President to fly—October 10 or 11, 1910—Theodore Roosevelt, then out of office, with Arch Hoxsey piloting a Wright Flier at a St. Louis flying meet.

Airplane flown from a ship—November 14, 1910—Eugene Ely flew a Curtiss Albany Flyer from an 83-foot platform on battleship USS *Birmingham.*

Licensed woman pilot—1911—Harriet Quimby earned FAI pilot license #37. She was also the first woman to fly across the English Channel on April 16, 1912, and the first woman to receive a piloting license from the Aero Club of America.

Airplane flown to a ship—January 10, 1911—Eugene Ely landed a Curtiss Albany Flyer on a platform on the USS *Pennsylvania,* moored in San Francisco Bay.

Naval Aviation Service created—May 8, 1911—With funds of $24,000 appropriated by Bureau of Navigation on March 4, 1911. This was also the date of the requisition of the U.S. Navy's first airplane, a Curtiss Model D to be delivered on July 1, 1911.

Military flight school—May 20, 1911—The Army established its pilot training school at College Park, Maryland, and bids were taken for hangars.

Transcontinental flight—September 17-November 5, 1911—Calbraith P. Rodgers flew 3,390 miles in 82 hours, 4 minutes over 49 days with 69 stops.

Official airmail delivery—September 23, 1911—Earl Ovington flew six miles from Long Island to Minneola, New York, for the first airmail delivery.

Parachute jump from an airplane—March 1, 1912—Army Captain Albert "Bert" Berry made a tethered parachute jump from an airplane at 3,500 feet over St. Louis, Missouri.

Aerial weaponry—June 7, 1912—A Lewis machine gun was test-fired by Army Captain C.D. Chandler from an Army Wright Model B in flight over College Park, Maryland.

Woman parachutist—June 21, 1913—18-year-old Georgia "Tiny" Broadwick made a tethered jump from 1,000 feet over Los Angeles, California.

Skywriting—July 19, 1913—Milton J. Bryant in Seattle, Washington.

Inside loop—November 18, 1913—Lincoln Beachey, who was also the first to fly upside-down in a custom-built Curtiss over Coronado, California. The first woman to loop was Ruth Law, in June 1915.

Scheduled airline using an airplane—January 1, 1914—Anthony Jannus piloted a flying boat from St. Petersburg to Tampa, Florida. One-way fare was $5.00. Contract ended March 30.

Naval Air Station—January 15-20, 1914—Pensacola was established as the permanent site after temporary camps at San Diego and Annapolis in 1911 and 1912.

National aircraft insignia—May 19, 1917—A white star with a red dot in its center on a blue circle, and vertical red, white, and blue stripes on the rudder was approved by the Army. This was temporarily replaced in February 1918 by a concentric red, white, and blue circle until the end of World War I.

Aerial combat—April 14, 1918—Air Service Lieutenants Douglas Campbell and Alan Winslow, 94th Pursuit Squadron; each downed one German plane.

National airmail service inaugurated—May 15, 1918—The Aviation Section of the Signal Corps established regular airmail service from Washington D.C. to Philadelphia to New York City.

Service combat ace—September 1918—Captain Eddie V. Rickenbacker, with a final victory total of 26. First victory on April 29, 1918 (eight days after the death of Manfred von Richthofen). First American combat ace outside of U.S. service was Captain Paul F. Baer, serving with Lafayette Escadrille.

Military transcontinental flight—December 4, 1918—Four Air Service Curtiss JN-4s left San Diego, California, but only one reached Jacksonville, Florida on December 22, 1918, piloted by Major Albert D. Smith.

Un-tethered, rip-cord parachute jump—April 28, 1919—Leslie L. Irvin made an un-tethered parachute jump at McCook Field in Dayton, Ohio, proving conclusively that one would not lose consciousness in a free-fall parachute jump, as had been predicted by some experts.

Scheduled airline with multiple destinations—May 1919—Motion picture director Cecil B. DeMille's Mercury Air Service in California had scheduled service to Santa Catalina Island and San Diego, and later to San Francisco. This airline was inaugurated five months before KLM began operations in Europe.

Transatlantic flight—May 16-31, 1919—U.S. Navy Lieutenant Commander Albert C. Read and pilot Lieutenant Walter Hinton flew 4,515 miles from Long Island to Plymouth, England, via Newfoundland, the Azores, and Lisbon in 53 hours, 58 minutes in a Curtiss NC-4.

Forestry air patrol—June 1, 1919—An organized and sustained aerial forest fire patrol using Curtiss JN-4Ds and JN-6Hs was initiated at Rockwell Field, California.

Army transcontinental reliability and endurance flight—October 8-31, 1919—New York to San Francisco and return. 44 aircraft completed the westbound leg, 15 completed the eastbound trip, and 10 completed the round-trip.

Scheduled international airline service—November 1, 1919—Aeromarine West Indies Airways, between Key West, Florida, and Havana, Cuba.

Altitude record—February 27, 1920—Army Major Rudolph W. "Shorty" Schroeder climbed 33,113 feet in a turbo-supercharged, Liberty-powered Packard-LePere airplane over McCook Field in Dayton, Ohio. This flight should also should qualify as the world's first vapor trail, as viewers on the ground reported everything from a passing comet to "a visitor from Mars."

Aerial law violation—April 27, 1920—Issued to Ormer Locklear for "reckless aerial driving" over Los Angeles. He was fined $25.00.

National Air Race—November 27, 1920—Mitchel Field, New York.

Transcontinental airmail service—February 22, 1921—Flown from Mineola, New York to San Francisco, California, in 23 hours and 20 minutes in a De Havilland DH-4M.

Pressurized military airplane—June 8, 1921—First flight of an Army Air Service pressurized cabin airplane, a DH–9A, piloted by Lieutenant Harold R. Harris.

Battleship sunk by airplanes—July 21, 1921—Joint service tests against the German battleship *Ostfriesland* ended dramatically when Brigadier General Billy Mitchell's army bombers dropped eleven 1000- and 2000-pound bombs, sinking the ship.

Crop dusting—August 4, 1921—5,000 catalpa trees were sprayed in 15 minutes in Troy, Ohio by a hopper-rigged Curtiss JN-4D piloted by Lieutenant John Macready with Etienne Dormoy.

Navy Bureau of Aeronautics established—August 10, 1921—Rear Admiral William A. Moffett was its first chief.

Aerial refueling—November 12, 1921—First air-to-air refueling, as such, was made when Wesley May stepped from the wing of one biplane to that of another with a five-gallon can of gasoline strapped to his back.

Aircraft carrier—March 20, 1922—USS *Langley* was converted from a coal-transporting ship to an aircraft carrier.

Helicopter in controlled horizontal flight—June 16, 1922—Henry Berliner flew a war-surplus Nieuport biplane fighter modified with a tilting tail rotor and a short-span upper wing with 14'0" helicopter blades at the tips, in a demonstration for the military at College Park, Maryland.

Aircraft carrier takeoff—October 17, 1922—U.S. Navy Lieutenant Virgil C. Griffin took off in a Vought VE–7SF from USS *Langley*, moored at York River, Virginia.

Speed record—October 18, 1922—Brigadier General William H. Mitchell became the first U.S. military pilot to hold the recognized speed record at 222.97 mph.

Aircraft carrier landing—October 26, 1922—USN Lieutenant Commander Godfrey Chevalier landed on the USS *Langley* in an Aeromarine 39-B. He was fatally injured in a crash two weeks later.

Transcontinental nonstop flight—May 2–3, 1923—Air Service Lieutenants Oakley G. Kelly and John A. Macready flew 2,500 miles nonstop from Roosevelt Field, New York to San Diego, California in 26 hours and 50 minutes in a Fokker T-2.

In-flight plane-to-plane refueling—June 27, 1923—Captain L.H. Smith and Lieutenant J.P. Richter refueled in-flight in an Army De Havilland DH-4B over Rockwell Field, San Diego. They also set a distance record of 3,293 miles covered in the flight.

Speed record—November 4, 1923—U.S. Navy Lieutenant Alford Williams flew at 266.59 mph in Navy-Curtiss Racer at Mitchel Field, Long Island, which remained a U.S. record until 1930.

Global flight—April 6-September 28, 1924—Four Douglas DWC World Cruisers commanded by Army Major F. Martin flew from and to Seattle, Washington. Only two planes completed the 26,345-mile flight of 371 hours, 11 minutes, at an average speed of 75 mph.

Altitude record—May 19, 1924—35,239 feet attained by Army Lieutenant John Macready in a LePere fighter over Dayton, Ohio.

Transcontinental dawn-to-dusk flight—June 23, 1924—Army Lieutenant Russell L. Maugham flew in a Curtiss PW-8 from New York to San Francisco with five fuel stops en route.

Scheduled air freight service—April 13, 1925—Implemented by auto manufacturer Henry Ford, between Detroit and Chicago.

Airplane over the North Pole—May 8–9, 1926—Admiral Richard E. Byrd, pilot Floyd Bennett, and a crew in the Fokker BA-1 *Josephine Ford*. There is controversy over Byrd's claim of a world record, with expressed doubts by Bernt Balchen (who also piloted

Byrd on the 1929 South Pole flight) and others, and more recent research suggests that he was well short of his goal when he turned back. Honors should instead go to Umberto Nobile and Roald Amundsen, who flew from Spitzbergen over the North Pole to Alaska a few days later.

Air Commerce Act—May 20, 1926—President Calvin Coolidge signed into law the first federal legislation regulating civil aeronautics.

Aerial reforesting—July 2, 1926—Seeding by airplane in Hawaii.

Army Air Corps established—July 2, 1926—Army Air Service restructured under the Air Corps Act.

Paratroops—1927—12 battle-ready marines successfully parachuted from a USMC transport plane in 14 seconds at Anacostia in Washington, D.C., and shortly afterward duplicated the feat by parachuting over the Potomac River with rubber rafts that were inflated during their descent.

Transatlantic solo flight—May 20–21, 1927—Charles A. Lindbergh flew from Long Island to Paris in 33 hours and 32 minutes in the *Spirit of St Louis.*

Transpacific flight—June 28–29, 1927—Army Lieutenants A.F. Hegenberger and Lester J. Maitland flew from Oakland, California to Honolulu, Hawaii in 25 hours and 49 minutes in a Fokker C-2 called *Bird of Paradise.*

Altitude record—July 25, 1927—U.S. Navy Lieutenant C. C. Champion climbed 38,484 feet in a Wright Apache.

Woman to cross the Atlantic by air—June 17-18, 1928—Amelia Earhart flew from Newfoundland to Wales as a passenger in a Fokker C–2 called *Friendship.*

Woman to fly transcontinental round-trip—August 31, 1928—Amelia Earhart on her "vagaboding trip" in an Avro Avian from Rye, New York to Glendale, California and return.

Autogiro flight—December 19, 1928—Harold F. Pitcairn in Willow Grove, Pennsylvania.

In-flight motion picture—Summer 1929—The first in-flight motion picture was shown on a Transcontinental Air Transport flight, where a demonstration consisted of a comedy short and a newsreel.

Transcontinental nonstop round-trip—August 15–21, 1929—Nick Mamer and Art Walker used air-to-air refueling to travel 7,200 point–to–point miles (or 10,000 air miles) from Spokane, Washington to New York City in a Buhl CA-6 Special called *Spokane Sun God.* Time aloft: 120 hours, 1 minute, 40 seconds.

Airplane over the South Pole—November 28-29, 1929—U.S. Navy Admiral Richard Byrd, pilot Bernt Balchen, radioman Harold June, and photographer A. C. McKinley flew over the South Pole in a Ford 4-AT called *Floyd Bennett.*

Woman's solo transcontinental flight—October 5-9, 1930—Laura Ingalls, in her De Havilland Gypsy Moth, from Roosevelt Field NY to Glendale CA with nine stops. Flight time: 30 hours, 27 minutes.

Transcontinental commercial air service—October 25, 1930—Between New York City and Los Angeles.

Autogiro altitude record—April 22, 1931—18,400 feet attained by Amelia Earhart.

Un-refueled endurance record—May 28, 1931—a Bellanca with Packard DR-980 diesel engine flew for 84 hours and 32 minutes without refueling, a record that has never been broken.

Rocket-powered, manned flight—June 4, 1931—William G. Swan, in a rocket-powered glider at Bader Field in Atlantic City, New Jersey. He also carried some pieces of mail, which would undoubtedly qualify this flight as the first rocket airmail.

Global flight—June 23-July 1, 1931—Wiley Post and Harold Gatty flew over 15,474 miles with 14 stops from and to Roosevelt Field, New York, in a Lockheed Vega. Flight time: 8 days, 15 hours, 51 minutes.

Transpacific nonstop flight—October 3, 1931—Clyde Pangborn and Hugh Herndon, Jr., flew 4,500 miles in 41 hours and 13 minutes from Sabishoro, Japan to Wenatchee, Washington.

Bendix Trophy—September 4, 1931—James H. Doolittle won the first Bendix transcontinental race flying a Laird Super Solution from Los Angeles to Cleveland in 9 hours and 10 minutes with an average speed of 223.058 mph. He then flew to New York to complete a full flight across the continent.

Solo blind flight—May 9, 1932—USAAC Captain A.F. Hegenberger flew solely on instruments without a check pilot aboard.

Transatlantic solo flight by a woman—May 20–21, 1932—Amelia Earhart flew 2,026 miles from Newfoundland to North Ireland in a Lockheed Vega 5B. Flight time: 14 hours and 56 minutes.

Transcontinental solo flight by a woman—August 25, 1932—Amelia Earhart flew 2,448 miles from Los Angeles to Newark in a Lockheed Vega 5B. Flight time: 19 hours and 15 minutes.

Presidential aircraft—1933—One USN Douglas RD-2 Dolphin was officially assigned for executive use by Franklin D. Roosevelt, but there is no record of him traveling in it, mainly due to his physical disability. It would be 10 more years before he flew in an airplane.

Global solo flight—July 15–22, 1933—Wiley Post flew 15,596 miles from and to Floyd Bennett Filed in New York in a Lockheed Vega 5 called *Winnie Mae.* Flight time: 7 days, 18 hours, 49 minutes, 30 seconds.

Bureau of Air Commerce—July 1, 1934—Established to replace the Aeronautics Branch in the Department of Commerce.

In-flight sound motion picture—Summer 1935—Central Airlines, en route from Washington, D.C. to Pittsburgh.

Transpacific scheduled airline—November 22, 1935—Pan American Airways, from Alameda on San Francisco Bay to Manila in the Martin M-130 *China Clipper.*

Aerial traffic report—1936—Broadcast from the Goodyear blimp over New York City.

Transcontinental speed record—January 13, 1936—Howard Hughes flew Jacqueline Cochran's Northrop Gamma 2G, modified with a 850hp Wright Cyclone engine, from Burbank, California to Newark, New Jersey in 9 hours and 27 minutes at an average speed of 259 mph, earning the Harmon Trophy.

Transatlantic round-trip flight—September 2-15, 1936—Henry T. "Dick" Merrill and Harry Richman flew 3,300 miles from New York to London in 18 hours and 38 minutes, and 2,300 miles from Southport to Newfoundland in 17 hours and 24 minutes in a Vultee V1-A called *Lady Peace.*

300-mph fighter plane—1937—Curtiss XP–37 attained 340 mph at 20,000 feet with new liquid-cooled Allison V-1710-C8 engine.

Global speed record—July 10–14, 1938—Howard Hughes and crew members Harry Connor, Ed Lund, Richard Stoddard, and Thomas Thurlow flew 14,791 miles from and to New York City in a in Lockheed 14. Flight time: 3 days, 19 hours, 9 minutes, 10 seconds.

Flight of a pressurized airliner—December 31, 1938—Boeing 307; the first one was put into regular use by TWA in April 1940.

Transcontinental speed record—February 11, 1939—USAAF Lieutenant Ben Kelsey flew a Lockheed XP-38 (in secrecy) from March Field in California to Mitchel Field in New York in 7 hours and 2 minutes, at an average speed of just under 400 mph. Kelsey caught a treetop on landing and crashed into a golf course sand trap, sustaining only minor injuries.

Transatlantic scheduled airline—May 20, 1939—Pan American Airways, from New York to Portugal and France, in a Boeing 314 *Yankee Clipper* (at first carried only airmail).

Autogiro airmail service—July 6, 1939—Eastern Air Lines, from Philadelphia Post Office to Camden New Jersey in a Kellett KD-1B.

Airplane to exceed 400 mph in level flight—October 1, 1940—Vought F4U Corsair; 404 mph.

Army Air Force established—June 20, 1941—Army Regulation 95-5 created the U.S. Army Air Force.

Civil Air Patrol established—December 1, 1941.

Aerial combat victory of World War II—December 7, 1941. The first aerial combat victory of the war was shared by USAAF 2nd Lieutenants Ken Taylor and George Welch of 5th Fighter Group, 47th Pursuit Squadron, both flying P-40Bs and scoring two victories over Japanese attackers near Oahu, Hawaii. Times were not recorded, so it is impossible to say who was first on the clock.

U.S. Army Air Force World War II combat ace—December 16, 1941—Lieutenant Boyd "Buzz" Wagner, flying a P-40.

Flying Tigers combat—December 20, 1941—The American Volunteer Group (Claire Chennault's Flying Tigers) in action over Kunming, China.

Naval battle fought entirely by airplanes—May 4–8, 1942. Battle of New Guinea, more popularly referred to as the Battle of the Coral Sea, was a strategic victory for the Allies, who used only aircraft to win the battle to ensure that naval vessels never came within gunshot range of Japanese ships.

U.S. Navy World War II combat ace—February 20, 1942—Lieutenant Edward "Butch" O'Hare flying an F4F.

U.S. attack on Japanese homeland—April 18, 1942—16 North American B-25s commanded by Lieutenant James H. Doolittle took off from USS *Hornet* and bombed Tokyo.

U.S. attack on Nazi Europe—July 4, 1942—Flown by B-17s of the 97th Bombardment Group against the Rouen-Sotteville rail yards in France. The first USAAF air raid on Germany was made by 8th Air Force B-17s against Wilhelmshaven and other targets in northeastern Germany on January 27, 1943.

Jet airplane—October 1, 1942—Bell XP-59A, piloted by Robert Stanley at Muroc Air Force Base in California.

President to fly while in office—January 11, 1943—Franklin Delano Roosevelt, in a Boeing 314 Clipper called *Dixie Clipper,* to Casablanca and back. (On the return trip, he celebrated his 65th birthday.) The first designated presidential aircraft, shortly thereafter, was a Consolidated C–87A Liberator Express.

Turbojet engine—March 1943—The Westinghouse X19A was the first American-designed turbojet engine.

Rocket airplane—July 5, 1944—The Northrop MX-334 was the first rocket airplane.

Nonstop flight over the North Pole—1944—USAF B-29 *Pacusan Dreamboat* flew from Honolulu to Cairo.

Carrier jet landing—November 6, 1945—U.S. Navy Ensign Jake C. West Ryan landed on the USS *Wake Island* in an FR-1. The landing was unplanned—the plane's piston engine failed and West came in powered only by the turbojet.

Carrier jet launch—July 21, 1946—Lieutenant Commander James Davidson made the first successful landings and takeoffs in an XFD Phantom (deck launched without catapults) on the USS *Franklin D. Roosevelt.*

Air Force established—September 18, 1947—With passage of the National Security Act, the U.S. Army Air Force became the U.S. Air Force, a separate military service.

Helicopter airmail service—October 1, 1947—Los Angeles Airways, Sikorsky S-51.

Airplane to break the sound barrier—October 14, 1947—Bell X-1, flown to Mach 1.06 (700 mph) by USAF Captain Charles E. Yeager at Muroc Air Force Base in California.

Nonstop global flight—March 2, 1949—Captain James Gallagher, Arthur Neal, and 12 crew members of the 43rd Bomb Group flew 23,452 miles in 94 hours and 1 minute with four aerial refuelings from and to Carswell Air Force Base in Texas in a Boeing B-50A called *Lucky Lady II*. For this, the 14-man crew became the first USAF recipients of the Mackay Trophy.

Transatlantic jet flight—September 22, 1950—USAF Colonel David C. Schilling flew 3,300 miles from England to the United States in 10 hours and 1 minute.

All-jet combat—November 8, 1950—Lieutenant Russell J. Brown Jr., piloting a Lockheed F-80C, shot down a MiG-15 during the Korean War.

Jet bomber—1951—Boeing's B-47, which rolled off the production line in Wichita, Kansas.

Jet ace—May 20, 1951—USAF Captain James Jabara, who shot down 15 enemy planes in Korea.

Helicopter to fly across the Atlantic—August 1, 1952—Two Sikorsky S-55s set not only this record, but the nonstop distance record for rotary-wing aircraft, as well, in flying 3,410 miles from Westover MA to Prestwick, Scotland in 42 hours and 25 minutes. Pilots were USAF Captain Vincent H. McGovern and Lieutenant Harold W. Moore.

President to solo an airplane—1953—Dwight D. Eisenhower, who soloed in 1937 while serving with General Douglas MacArthur in the Philippines and received his pilot's license in July 1939. Eisenhower was also the first to have a presidential helicopter in 1957. The first president as an active pilot was George H. Bush, who flew combat missions in a USN Grumman TBF during World War II. Neither, however, pursued a career in aviation. George W. Bush was first president qualified as jet pilot as a member of the Texas Air National Guard.

Airplane to exceed Mach 2—November 20, 1953—A. Scott Crossfield flew a Douglas D-558-2 at Mach 2.435 at Edwards Air Force Base in California.

Speed record—December 12, 1953—USAF Major Charles Yeager flew a Bell X-1A at 1,600 mph.

Aerial refueling of a jet aircraft—September 1, 1954—Boeing B-47 bomber by a KB-47B tanker.

Transcontinental round-trip flight in one day—May 21, 1955—USAF Lieutenant John M. Conroy flew 5,085 miles from New York City to Los Angeles and back in a North American F-86. Flight time: 11 hours, 22 minutes, 27 seconds.

Altitude record—September 7, 1956—Captain Iven C. Kincheloe piloted a Bell X-2 to an altitude of 126,000 feet at more than 1,500 mph, for which he was awarded the 1956 Mackay Trophy. The record stands in a separate category as a rocket-powered aircraft altitude flight, excluding dedicated spacecraft.

President to use a helicopter—1957—Dwight D. Eisenhower, in a Bell H–13J.

Global nonstop jet flight—January 17-18—USAF Major General Archie J. Olds, Jr. led a flight of three Boeing B-52s on a 24,325-mile journey around the world in 45 hours and 19 minutes at an average speed of 525 mph.

Supersonic woman—May 18, 1957—Jacqueline Cochran flew a Canadair North American F-86 faster than the speed of sound.

NASA formed—October 1, 1958—National Aeronautics and Space Administration replaces NACA.

Endurance record—December 4, 1958—John Cook and Robert Timm took off from McCarran Airfield in Las Vegas, Nevada, in a Cessna 172 and, with in-flight refueling, remained aloft for 64 days, 22 hours, 19 minutes, and 5 seconds—more than two months in continual flight. They finally landed at McCarren on February 7, 1959.

Domestic jet passenger service—December 10, 1958—National Airlines route between New York City and Miami, Florida.

Highest parachute jump—August 16, 1960—USAF Captain Joseph W. Kittinger parachuted from 102,800 feet over New Mexico. He wore a pressure suit and was carried to that altitude in a balloon gondola. It took 1 hour and 43 minutes to reach altitude, and only 13 minutes and 45 seconds to make the return trip. He also set three other records at the same time: (1) the highest man had ever gone in unpowered flight, (2) the longest free fall in history—16 miles, and (3) the first man to exceed the speed of sound without an aircraft—614 mph during free fall.

Commercial airliner to exceed the speed of sound—April 1962—Douglas DC-8-53, in service with Philippine Airlines, exceeded the speed of sound during a brief dive.

Solo global flight by a woman—1964—Geraldine "Jerrie" Mock, in a Cessna 180 called *The Spirit of Columbus.*

Transcontinental carrier-to-carrier flight—June 6, 1967—USN Captain Robert Dose and Lieutenant Commander Paul Miller flew a Vought F8U Crusader from the USS *Bonhomme Richard* in the Pacific to the USS *Saratoga* in the Atlantic in 3 hours and 28 minutes.

Female airline pilot—January 29, 1973—Emily H. Warner, as second officer on a Frontier Airlines Boeing 737.

Female U.S. Navy pilot—February 27, 1974—Lieutenant Barbara Ann Allen, at the Naval Air Station in Corpus Christi, Texas.

Female U.S. Air Force test pilot—June 10, 1989—Captain Jacquelyn S. Parker, who graduated from the Air Force Test Pilot School at Edwards Air Force Base in California.

Computer-designed commercial aircraft—June 12, 1994—Boeing 777-200 first flown.

Female bomber pilot—March 31, 1995—2nd Lieutenant Kelly Flinn began training at Barksdale Air Force Base and graduated on September 25; she was assigned to fly a B-52 Stratofortress.

Jet pilot who became U.S. President—2001—George W. Bush, Texas Air National Guard.

Gaffney, Timothy R. *Chuck Yeager: First Man to Fly Faster Than Sound.* Chicago: Children's Press, 1986.

Hallion, Richard. *Test Pilots: The Frontiersmen of Flight.* Washington, D.C.: Smithsonian Institution Press, 1988.

Levinson, Nancy. *Chuck Yeager: The Man Who Broke the Sound Barrier.* New York: Walker, 1988.

Lundgren, William R. *Across the High Frontier.* New York: Morrow, 1955.

Napier, Peggy. "Chuck E. Yeager: Supersonic Flight Pioneer," *West Virginia History,* Volume 40 (1978-1979): 293-303.

Rotundo, Louis C. *Into the Unknown: The X-1 Story.* Washington, D.C.: Smithsonian Institution Press, 1994.

Yeager, Chuck, and Leo Jaons (Editor). *Yeager: An Autobiography.* New York: Bantam Books, 1986.

Yeager, Chuck, and Charles Leersen. *Press on: Further Adventures in the Good Life.* New York: Bantam Books, 1988.

Books

Gaffney, Timothy R. *Chuck Yeager: First Man to Fly Faster Than Sound.* Chicago: Children's Press, 1986.

Levinson, Nancy. *Chuck Yeager: The Man Who Broke the Sound Barrier.* New York: Walker, 1988.

Maynard, Christopher, and David Jeffries. *Air Battles/Air Combat in World War II.* London, New York: Franklin Watts, Inc., 1987.

Smith, Elizabeth Simpson. *Coming Out Right: The Story of Jacqueline Cochran, the first woman aviator to break the sound barrier.* New York: Walker & Co. Library, 1991.

Wolfe, Tom. *The Right Stuff.* New York: Farrar Straus & Giroux, 1983.

Stein, R. Conrad. *Chuck Yeager Breaks the Sound Barrier.* New York: Children's Press, 1987.

Websites

Academy of Achievement
www.achievement.org

American Aces of World War II
www.acepilots.com/usaaf_yeager.html

C.E. "Bud" Anderson.com
www.cebudanderson.com

Chuck Yeager.com
www.chuckyeager.com

EAA Young Eagles
www.youngeagles.org

Edwards Air Force Base
Afftc.Edwards.af.mil

NASA Headquarters
www.hq.nasa.org

X-1 Photo Collection
www.dfrc.nasa.gov/gallery/photo/X-1/

Movies

The Right Stuff, by Philip Kaufman, 1983.

Apollo 13, by Ron Howard, 1995.

page:

7: Courtesy NASA
12: © Bettmann/Corbis
14: © Bettmann/Corbis
17: © Corbis
22: © Bettmann/Corbis
24: © KJ Historical/Corbis
29: © Corbis
33: © Bettmann/Corbis
35: © Hulton-Deutsch Collection/Corbis
40: © Bettmann/Corbis
43: © Lake County Museum/Corbis
44: © Bettmann/Corbis
47: © Bill Ross/Corbis
50: Courtesy NASA
58: © Bettmann/Corbis
60: © Bettmann/Corbis
63: © Bettmann/Corbis
65: © Bettmann/Corbis
70: Courtesy NASA
73: © James L. Amos/Corbis
77: © Bettmann/Corbis

Cover: Courtesy NASA, photo by Lt. Robert A. Hoover

Cover inset and Frontis: © Philip Gendreau/Corbis

Colleen Madonna Flood Williams is the wife of Paul R. Williams and mother of Dillon Joseph Meehan. She has a Bachelor's Degree in Elementary Education with a minor in Art. She is the daughter of Patrick and Kathleen Flood. Colleen is the author of more than ten educational children's books, as well as numerous poems, magazine articles, and other writings.